Do Agile

Futureproof your mind.
Stay grounded.

Tim Drake

In memory of my brother John.
A wonderful one-off.

Published by
The Do Book Company 2020
Works in Progress Publishing Ltd
thedobook.co

Text © Tim Drake 2020
Illustration © Gavin Strange 2020
Author photograph
© Jonathan Cherry 2020

To find out more about our company,
books and authors, please visit
thedobook.co or follow us **@dobookco**

5% of our proceeds from the sale of
this book is given to The Do Lectures
to help it achieve its aim of making
positive change: **thedolectures.com**

Cover designed by James Victore
Book designed and set by Ratiotype

Printed and bound by OZGraf Print
on Munken, an FSC-certified paper

A CIP catalogue record for this book
is available from the British Library

ISBN 978-1-907974-80-9

10 9 8 7 6 5 4 3 2

Contents

Prologue

Mahatma Gandhi was unlike most political activists of the time. His Hindu beliefs led him to a form of political activism that was non-violent. Even after the Massacre of Amritsar in 1919, where nearly 400 defenceless Indians were gunned down, he shunned violence.

Of his many remarkable qualities, perhaps the two most outstanding were his courageous resilience and his independence of mind. He saw things clearly. He was profoundly autonomous, and not influenced by the received thinking of his era.

He had what we would now call a growth mindset. Unlike a fixed mindset — which is defensive, resistant to change, and unable to acknowledge that things move on — the growth mindset is flexible, responds positively to change and relishes new ideas.

Gandhi inspired and led resistance in two countries, India and previously in South Africa. In both countries the leaders had developed extremely fixed mindsets that had evolved to protect those in power — the white ruling minority. By taking on such powerful forces, particularly in India, Gandhi was able to reboot the thinking of vast swathes of the population. He enabled them to see what was possible — and the action that would deliver it.

The momentum built up by his policy of non-violent non-cooperation was achieved by convincing Indians, through example, that it wasn't British guns that were keeping them enslaved, but their own thinking. His great achievement was to unshackle that thinking. By enabling them to reframe their perceptions of how society could, and should, be ordered, he unleashed enormous energy and enthusiasm for reform.

The enthusiasm for his approach was intensified by the fact that he was tapping into a powerful moral code of conduct, underpinned by the country's Hindu beliefs in non-violence. The combination of the reframing of the context — demonstrating through personal example that non-violent non-cooperation worked — and rooting it in a resonating moral core, made it a force that ultimately the British colonialists could not resist.

The world we live in today may not require the epic scale of Gandhi's unshackling of the mindsets of a nation to provide a new perception of how a country could be run. Or maybe it does. But it could transform your perception of how a wider, more relevant reality could radically improve your potential to grow and flourish.

We need to remain mentally agile and open to the idea of updating and reframing our thinking. By carrying out mental reboots, we retain our autonomy and objectivity. The aim of this book is to show you why it's necessary and how it's done.

I will never let anyone walk through
my mind with their dirty feet.

Mahatma Gandhi

It's not an adventure until something goes wrong.

Yvon Chouinard, founder of Patagonia

Introduction

Some years ago, I stood on the platform at Cannon Street underground station in a state of shock. A sense of profound loss numbed my mind.

A train came in, and I stepped aboard, not caring where it went. As it clattered noisily through the tunnel towards the first stop, I looked around at the other people in the carriage. How were they so calm? Didn't they realise the normal world was in suspension? The doors opened at the next stop. And closed again. Slowly, my brain started to awaken from its frozen state. I had a young family at home. They would need me. Not only now, but into the foreseeable future.

Slowly I was coming to terms with the fact that I had just signed away my previously very successful company for £1.

With no monthly pay cheque or future pension, I knew that I would need to completely reset my thinking in order to dig myself out of this hole. I needed to become unstuck. Fast.

Taking stock and drawing on all my mental reserves, I knew I had a good track record. I had left a senior job in marketing to set up a sports-shoe business with a colleague some fourteen years previously. It was the first specialist business of its kind in the UK, and soon grew to become a chain of over forty shops.

We were then hit by three blows. The first was a major fashion change. It was the early 90s and, believe it or not, the trainer as a leisure shoe suddenly went out of fashion. Sales dropped dramatically. I saw evidence of this one day when travelling on a crowded train. Looking around, I couldn't see one person wearing trainers.

The second was an increase in competition. The main high street retailers entered the market just as it was contracting. They quickly absorbed what little demand there was for fashion trainers. And the third blow was the severe recession of 1992. Spending dropped and, to make things worse, our bank got into financial difficulties. As a result, it attempted to withdraw loans from customers like us, just when we needed the money.

I was very much down, but I certainly wasn't out. With my background in marketing, I already knew that my experience might be of value to the industry as a whole. I did some gap analysis — just as I had done when we started the business to identify the broader opportunity for sports shoes.

Soon enough, a possible solution struck me. My now neutral status meant that I could now look at the industry as an outsider. My idea was simple enough, but hadn't been done before: to set up a forum bringing together chief executives from competing companies to share ideas, identify problems and find solutions.

It would be a subscription-based forum for leaders only, that would allow them to speak in confidence with their industry peers. It would meet three or four times a year — MDs are busy — and would contain both fashion brands *and* retailers. This was unprecedented as normally the two sides only met to haggle over prices and discounts. But with so many rivals within earshot, it already meant that issues such as cartels and price fixing would not be possible. By looking at the overall supply chain in a new way, everyone could see things differently.

Importantly it was collaborative, not confrontational. A further move forward for the industry. We invited outside experts to offer different perspectives. We encouraged a sense of conviviality by holding the meetings over dinner. It felt as much a social gathering as a business one. Once, we even had a legal case settled over the dessert course.

It may have been too late for my own business but my hope was that this initiative would allow others to futureproof theirs. In doing so, not only was I able to bring new thinking to the industry in which I operated, but I was able to create a new business — and, importantly, start to earn some income.

Something must have been right about the thinking. Over two decades later the forum continues to thrive. I was even approached by two other industries to set up similar initiatives. They have also been successful, and continue to grow and evolve to this day.

I share this story to illustrate that I had to adapt my mindset while staying true to my values and beliefs. This adaptation was not instant. However agile you are mentally, it sometimes takes time to rethink how you perceive the reality around you. And this is what underlies the thinking in the book. It examines how our mindset needs to be constantly examined, updated and refreshed. The way we have always thought may be comfortable, but it can also be risky. In an increasingly complex world, we need to keep our thinking relevant and agile, and if it isn't, to actively reboot our minds to ensure that it is. Let's get started.

**The difficulty lies not in new ideas,
but escaping old ones.**

John Maynard Keynes

1
Understanding Mindsets

Mindsets are what we all have, whether we are aware of them or not. And more often than not, we are blissfully unaware of them.

Back in the 1930s, a female relative of great ability and energy was working in Whitehall. As a senior civil servant, she earned twice as much as her fiancé. When she married, she had to resign from her job to raise a family, often struggling on their single, lower income. There was never any question of her going back to work after having children.

Twenty-five years later, her daughter had a job as head of the French Department at a grammar school in Sussex. When she had her first child in 1965, she had to resign, with no job to return to. It was the Swinging Sixties, but before maternity leave existed.

Years later, both women were horrified that they had given up such senior, hard-won positions without a second thought. But it was the system, and it wasn't questioned at the time. It had always been that way. It was just the way things were.

These are examples, from the relatively recent past, of how mindset can determine how we think, behave and act in ways we *think* are acceptable and normal, but which, in different circumstances or with different perspectives, appear absurd and even wrong.

Mindsets are complex things, made up of attitudes, values and beliefs. Some change over time, and some don't. The ones that don't can become 'set'. We believe they are normal and that's how the world sees things. Most of us think we are open-minded and our views are reasonable, because that is how the majority of the people around us think. But the truth is that we may be wrong. The world can change around us without us realising.

A few years ago, I co-wrote a book called *You Can Be as Young as You Think* with social scientist Chris Middleton. One of our key findings was that you can have either a young or old outlook on life, whatever your age. Studies showed that some people's attitudes started 'ageing' at a remarkably young age, some as early as eighteen.

Conversely, we found that there was a hard core of older people — around 20 per cent of respondents — whose attitudes were open to growing and adapting as they got older. Significantly, that's only one in five people who, throughout their lives, remained mentally agile and open to change. We called each group Old Brains and Young Brains.

Most of us would like to think of ourselves as Young Brains. I know I do. But even those of us who think we are open to fresh thinking have blind spots. I still trip myself up from time to time. And, as I will show, I had a couple of mindsets that were painfully outdated.

The influencers of mindset

There are three major influencers on our mindsets:

— **the environment we live in** — including politics, society, the media

— **our relationships with other people**, especially those close to us

— **our inner voice** or 'self-talk'

Let's look at them.

1. Our environment

We cannot help but be influenced by the culture we live in, the politics of the time, and the media we consume. Whether we live in a religious or secular society, a totalitarian regime or a liberal democracy, our perceptions and attitudes to life in general — and specific mindsets — will be affected.

As the media we access (if we are free to access it) continues to fragment and polarise, we increasingly live in our own bubble. The social media groups we join, Twitter accounts we follow or print media we consume can often reflect our own views and opinions. We find it comfortable reading, particularly when the fury we may feel on a particular issue is reflected. Shamefully, we are often looking for vindication rather than an antidote. However, the outcome is that we are closing down our own thinking, without even realising it.

2. Other people and relationships

We are a social species. In the words of Hilary Cottam, the author and social entrepreneur, 'Relationships — the simple human bonds between us — are the foundation of good lives. They bring us joy, happiness and a sense of possibility.'

As multiple research studies have shown, having positive relationships with those around us is the single most important factor in our happiness and sense of wellbeing.

We should be grateful, not just for the enjoyment of those relationships, but for the feeling of balance they bring. If our lives and minds are on an even keel it is much easier to be agile. And being agile means we have a mindset that is positive and ready for action. We can be swift and creative because we have an inner confidence, instead of self-doubt or feelings of vulnerability from our lack of positive relationships.

At the same time, being open with ourselves about any difficulties in our relationships with those close to us is one of the hardest things to do, but may bring considerable benefits.

If you don't admit to yourself the seriousness of the effects of 'toxic' people in your life, things can fester and become worse over time. Futureproofing your mind is one of the themes of this book, and it is made far more challenging if part of your mind is processing the effects of such poison. It keeps you rooted in the pain of the here and now. Resolving, and possibly ending, a toxic relationship can be difficult for all concerned in the short term, but longer term, it may be the best course of action. And you will be able to become unstuck and move on.

However challenging, it's important to stay calm and keep listening. It is worth remembering the old adage: find out how your enemy thinks so you can fight them better. By being aware of how they think and feel, you are not only better informed about how to deal with them, but you may learn something that will help you resolve the situation in a less painful way. In all areas of difficult personal relationships, opening up communications may highlight the facts and ideas that can facilitate a possibly quicker and less damaging resolution.

So be open and honest with yourself. Be aware of and cherish your enriching relationships and networks. And tackle any that are debilitating.

3. Our inner voice

Our inner narrator defines both the story of ourselves that we live every day and our role in that story. So it is crucial that the story we hear is positive, and not one that talks down our performance and contribution at every turn.

It's unhelpful that the pressures of modern living — squeezed time, keeping up with the latest technologies and trends, and the value placed on appearances — can make this more of a challenge. And as the outside world might appear to be getting less understanding and sympathetic, it can be very easy to let negative thinking and negative self-talk creep in.

Addressing this is a constant process. We need to continually find methods to avoid listening for too long or too frequently to the voice that tells us we are no good, that we are imposters who are in imminent danger of exposure. It is estimated that Imposter Syndrome — a phrase coined by psychologists way back in 1978 — is something 75 per cent of people suffer from.

So, we all need to develop tools that lift us out of negative mindsets. We need to exercise self-compassion — not to give in to any temptation to beat ourselves up. We need to generate positive mindsets that are life-enhancing, not life-reducing. Only then can we thrive, and positively engage with a rapidly changing world.

Learning points and To Do list

Environment:

1. See the bigger picture. You are not always right.

2. Stay widely informed by sampling a website, podcast or discussion forum that features viewpoints that don't correspond with your own. Your current worldview may need to adapt or evolve.

3. Keep this broad-based, but from time to time dive deeper into specific areas of personal interest — global political trends, populist movements, poverty etc.

Personal relationships:

1. Work hard at sustaining and enhancing your friendships and connection to relatives. This will require time, and kindness.

2. Acknowledge when a relationship is becoming counterproductive for both parties and plan the best solution. Any action you take should be responsible and empathetic.

The inner voice:

1. Know you are a positive and worthwhile human being.

2. Constantly be aware of your inner voice and exercise self-compassion to ensure it is reset to positive if negative self-talk creeps in.

3. Constantly monitor your environment, and don't let negativity impact on your mood even when surrounded by it.

You will notice, by the way, that the first statement on our environment — uniquely — is negative. This underlines the need to admit your current thinking may be wrong. You may be still caught in a mindset that is outdated. Humility is all. We need to guard against our own assumptions that how we see the world is, by definition, the one correct view.

The fact that an opinion is widely held is no evidence whatever that it is not utterly absurd.

—

Bertrand Russell

2
Openness and Neoteny

We may think we are open-minded, but the facts tell a different story. Studies show that attitudes start ageing from our late teens and continue through to old age, and are consistent across geographies.

This is also confirmed by studies in evolutionary biology. Neoteny is the term evolutionary biologists use. It means the retention of adolescent features into adulthood. Juveniles in species tend to be more adaptive and flexible than adults, and thus more effective, especially in new situations. This is because more conservative perspectives have yet to be developed. Plasticity is still possible in thinking and coping with the surrounding environment, because rigidity of thinking has not yet set in.

How old you are, who you associate with, your family situation, how your relationships are evolving, are all factors that will impact on your outlook, and how young it stays. And as a result, how enthusiastically you now engage in new experiences.

Without openness there is no autonomy

I had two wake-up calls which showed me that I had become stuck in outdated mindsets, and that I needed to unshackle myself, and move on.

Both were related to sexual orientation and identity. They occurred at a time when society was still closed off to sexual differences. I was in my twenties and working in an advertising agency. This was the 1970s and while homosexuality had been decriminalised, it was still not openly discussed. I was returning from a business meeting on a train one day and a colleague mentioned that our boss was homosexual. Looking back on it now, I cannot for the life of me understand how profoundly gobsmacked I was.

I had huge respect for him. He was intellectually brilliant, an excellent businessman and a very kind human being. And I liked him enormously. So, based on my reaction, I had some rethinking to do.

As it happens, I was ready for a mindset change. Around this time, I had started to read Armistead Maupin's *Tales of the City* — a series of books about the gay scene in San Francisco, rich in humour and humanity. I loved the stories. The characters they featured were colourful and engaging. So the combination of my boss, who I respected deeply, being gay, and Maupin's brilliant chronicles of the gay scene in California, helped to completely recalibrate my mindset.

The second wake-up call came not long after. My wife and I would regularly meet friends in a pub on a Monday night. One was a very successful salesman for a large computer company, an ex-rugby player and the father of two children. One day, he started growing his blond hair long, which seemed out of character.

He disappeared for some months, phoning to make excuses. When he finally reappeared, he was a woman. To say we were surprised was an understatement. It transpired that he had always believed he had been inhabiting the wrong body, but now felt released, infinitely more comfortable and content with his new physical and mental identity.

We were supportive, but as we sipped our drinks we were all struggling to come to terms with the new situation. Fortunately, resolution was at hand. One of our companions, a bear of a man, stood up, leant across the table, and kissed our friend on the lips.

The impact was extraordinary. Our transgender friend suddenly changed in our minds. *He* instantly became *her*. This one act of openness and kindness had transformed the situation. Again, my thinking had been unstuck.

Both these anecdotes served as a jolt. I realised I had gone along with the mainstream assumptions of the time on these issues of sexual identity. This was ironic, because I thought I was open-minded, but in both cases, I had been shocked because the reality was that I was very much stuck in the groupthink of the time.

The lesson for me was that without genuine openness — and continual self-examination of that openness — I had retained prejudices without even realising. I thought I was in control of how I perceived the world. But the reality was that my thinking was not aligned with genuine autonomy. My mindset was that of the conventional thinkers — and media — that surrounded me.

Updating mindsets

Updating mindsets can sometimes take time. It requires both a programme (see the To Do lists at the end of each chapter) and some application. Sometimes there are lightbulb moments, like there were for me in the above examples, but generally it demands some conscious and considered thinking.

One opportunity is to consciously develop a mindset that takes account of the principle of neoteny. And to do that you need to look at how younger people are thinking. Looking at the attitudes of younger age cohorts can give insights into a more relevant way to address some of the challenges evolving in society today.

Young people approach life with fluidity. This is a very relevant response to the pace and unpredictability of events in our work and business lives. This can be anxiety-inducing for people with relatively fixed mindsets, who resist change and flexibility. But for people who are aiming to keep — or develop — a more open mindset, it is an opportunity to be more adaptive, and respond positively to events.

Life is filled with ambiguity, so getting stressed when things don't turn out as you expect wastes both time and energy. This does not mean you abandon your moral compass. You retain a clear idea of what is right or wrong. But you abandon the fixed mindset position of believing that *I'm right and you're wrong.*

This is the essence of being agile. Your thinking is flexible and your responses are rapid, but you check that you are right before you move on. Right in the sense both of being correct, and of being grounded in sound principles. It's just that you understand that the world is excitingly fluid, and that the rigidities of the past are unhelpful.

Dare to dream

Regular checking that you are practising neoteny in this sense will help to confirm that your mindset is retaining its openness. Another attitude of young people confirmed by research is their tendency to have dreams of future possibilities. Experience-hardened, more closed mindsets tend to have a belief that dreams don't always come true. They fear failure.

Open mindsets are more fearless. They take risk as a motivator to achieve great things. Change and fluidity offer an opportunity to be creative, to invent new solutions. Tomorrow can be better than today. An open mindset would never articulate the words, 'That's been tried. It didn't work.'

An uplifting example of this is Greta Thunberg and Extinction Rebellion. The movement she supercharged with her directness and articulacy is challenging attitudes on climate change across the world. Thinking clearly, as a young person, gave her the courage to dream. Her dream stripped away all the excuses of why reducing carbon emissions quickly was too difficult — the only strategy was to hope a technical solution would come up before the glaciers melted and the world was drowned in the chaos of rising sea levels.

She had a child's clarity that stopping the slide to global human extinction is achievable if decisive action is taken now. The movement is unapologetic in communicating the truth that if decisive action is taken immediately, climate change can be halted before it is too late. The power of her dream, and her arguments for the solutions, have been embraced by people of all ages. This is neoteny writ large.

Enhancing mindsets

Both growth and fixed mindsets have superchargers.

The superchargers are the attitudes and beliefs rooted in the psychologies of optimism and pessimism. The power of positivity will be dealt with at several points in the book. Optimism is a powerful driver in the open mindset. It enables openness to opportunity to be transformed into productive action. Energy that can be put into new opportunities, rather than defending the past.

Pessimism, on the other hand, plays an important role in closing down mindsets. It shuts the door on openness. Pessimism is bad news on all fronts. Chief among them is the concomitant of pessimism — what psychologists call 'learned helplessness'. Believing that nothing is powerful enough to significantly alter the world around them, pessimists are frozen by a feeling of paralysis at their sense of ineffectiveness.

The psychological evidence clearly shows that pessimists achieve less, give up earlier, and get depressed more regularly. OK, optimists may sometimes be unrealistic in what they can achieve, but surely it's better to be slightly unrealistic and achieve something, than to be pessimistic and achieve nothing.

In rethinking a mindset it is important to be patient. It can sometimes take time for emotional buy-in to catch up with how your mind now sees things. And without emotional commitment the results may be less profound, and less sustainable.

Learning points and To Do list

1. Make an honest appraisal of yourself in terms of neoteny. How adaptable and flexible are you — especially in new, unfamiliar situations?

2. Concentrate on fluidity in challenging situations, and conquer fears of ambiguity. Understand that total clarity may be desirable, but probably not achievable.

3. Focus every day on improving the openness of your mindset, while being rigorous in evaluating what is true and what is relevant.

4. Reflect before acting, so your reaction to events is agile, but not impulsive or knee-jerk.

5. Dare to dream. Look for hints and insights that might, at some point, build into an uplifting vision of what you might achieve. And then commit to the dream.

If my mind can conceive it,
if my heart can believe it —
then I can achieve it.

—

Muhammad Ali

3
Getting Fit for Your Purpose(s)

Part of being agile is the ability to bounce back when events knock you for six. In sport, in work, in society, in relationships — you name it, life has setbacks, usually just when you don't want them. To quote Claudius in *Hamlet*, 'When sorrows come, they come not single spies, but in battalions.' We need strong defences to cope, and move on. And mental resilience is one defence we all need.

The American Psychological Association (APA) defines mental resilience as the process of adapting well in the face of adversity, trauma, tragedy, threats and sources of stress. Simply said, it is about having the mental strength to deal with pressures and challenges.

Psychologists are in agreement that to build mental strength you need to focus on an individual's ability to build a sense of control of their own emotions — and have confidence in that control. This, they say, is rooted in people being comfortable in their own skin and, crucially, in having a life purpose. Having a life purpose means they are sure of who they are, and have a strong moral code that gives them a clear perspective of events unfolding around them. They can be confident their response will be aligned with this code, and take strength from the knowledge they are doing the right thing. Self-respect then follows.

The basic building blocks of good health — exercise, diet and sleep — are also vital in building mental resilience. Meditation can also be helpful. These all help build stamina (both physical and mental) and the balance of mind that aids perspective. Gratitude, too, can be an important element in resilience. Being grateful for the good things you have going for you is a strong antidote to whatever peace of mind you may have just lost.

Also high on the APA list is fostering a positive mental attitude. We will look more closely at this in Chapter 8. It's worth noting that in taking up a positive attitude, its opposite doesn't automatically dissipate. It still takes effort to avoid strength-sapping and debilitating pessimism. As was argued earlier, pessimism leads to learned helplessness. The reverse of resilience.

Despite having to sell my company, Cobra Sports, for £1, I had been confident in my purpose. That purpose had been to build a chain of sports-shoe shops that achieved two aims. The first was our broader company aim: to get more people participating in and enjoying sport by providing highly informed and trustworthy advice to customers on the right shoe for their needs (gait, pronation, and level of seriousness). Although hard to believe now, there were no shops that did this, and certainly none on the high street. The second aim was more personal: to have highly trained and articulate staff to provide that trustworthy advice. A team that could be proud of their expertise and the help they were giving.

Twenty years after Cobra Sports folded, my daughter was wearing an old sweatshirt with our logo splashed across the front. The security guard at the shopping centre she was headed for stopped her as she approached. She was slightly worried, but he soon reassured her, explaining that he'd worked for us. He said it was the happiest and most motivating job he'd ever had. I like to believe this was because we had a purpose — one shared by the whole team of 200 employees.

Adapting purposes

It had been a worthwhile purpose, and it had worked. But it was no longer relevant to me, as the business was gone. It taught me that life events mean adapting one's purpose and refocusing in response to those events.

If you have already known your purpose from a very young age, and it's one that will stay the course, you can treat this chapter as revision. If not, you are far from alone. Indeed, most people find that over a lifetime their purpose adapts to the values that are relevant to them at the time, usually in response to life events. Having a purpose that adapts and alters is not unusual and can be a more attainable prospect than finding 'one true calling' and sticking with it.

It is the reason for the plural 'purpose(s)' in the chapter heading. Far too much emphasis is placed on finding your one true purpose and it's incredibly unhelpful. It puts too much pressure on finding that one glistening gem and hinders you from the multiple ways you could feel fulfilled over the course of a lifetime.

The crucial thing is to make sure any adaptations are made within the overall framework of your long-term moral principles and (as we shall see, within that) the values most relevant — and motivating — to you.

The focus of my subsequent purpose evolved slowly.

But over time, I have refined it to: 'helping people get insight into their situation so they can be more effective and fulfil more of their potential'. All the activities I now pursue — and have done for over two decades — are underpinned by this purpose. Whether it's writing books, speaking at conferences, running CEO think tanks, being actively involved in charities, they are all aligned with my purpose. It's not tidy and precise, but it's accurate, and true. Above all, it motivates me to keep on working well beyond conventional retirement age.

A strong moral code

> There comes a time when one must take a position that is neither safe, nor politic, nor popular, but we must do it because Conscience tells us it is right.

Martin Luther King

What has helped me significantly through the vicissitudes of being self-employed, with no monthly salary cheque and other challenges along the way, has been the key element — confirmed by the studies into mental resilience — of possessing a strong moral code.

My moral code is based on honesty, compassion, fairness and kindness. They may sound like good, wholesome values, found in any mushy fairytale, but they can be very hard to live up to at times. And if you want to listen to conscience, which tells you something isn't right, you have to find some mental resilience to retain your integrity and self-respect.

Conscience is an element of the human mind, validated by both philosophers and psychologists. It's something you feel as well as understand intellectually. As we'll see, it applies to all four of my foundational principles. Let's look at why I try to live by them.

Honesty

Being honest with yourself is just as important as being honest with other people. This is especially true with work. I well remember working with a company who hired an alarmingly ruthless chief executive, who subsequently spent time in prison. I had to deal with someone working for him who had accepted his code of morality. He, like others I have met in my career, tried to convince himself that living by one set of values at work, and another set in his private life, was OK.

It's not OK, and never will be. Eventually the double standards destroy the integrity of the individual. Mental health and self-respect issues reduce the individual to a shadow of what they would have been if they had stayed honest. Conscience monitors honesty, and ensures honesty is something you feel in your belly as much as understand up in your head.

In terms of the message of this book, it is thus central to being agile — without it you are in danger of being nimble, but having no solid basis to move from, or to. And without solid and sustainable foundations, you won't feel grounded.

Most importantly, it is vital to futureproofing — a dishonest construct for a future is one likely to implode through lack of substance.

Compassion

Compassion means not only being sympathetic to suffering, but having a desire to alleviate it. This is especially relevant to one of the major trends of the last decade, namely a growing tendency to see the less fortunate members of society as scroungers, whose misfortunes are self-inflicted, rather than the result of poor housing, education and poverty. This is partly driven by self-interest and selfishness — an unwillingness to share resources — and partly by ignorance — a lack of understanding and empathy for those suffering deprivation and the reduction of the little support they had.

Conscience again comes into play. We feel as well as know that action is required to be more compassionate, whenever we get the opportunity.

Fairness

Life is not fair, but that doesn't mean we have licence to behave unfairly.

Fairness again has its roots in conscience. We feel, as well as know, that if fairness underpins our actions they will be just, and we will be able to act without guilt. It should govern all behaviour, because unfairness is not only unjust, it ultimately destabilises society, so we all lose.

Kindness

Whereas compassion is about being empathetic to human suffering, kindness is the generous response to human beings around you. It is often insightful — foreseeing someone's discomfort before it happens. It is about being proactive in a good-natured, benign and affectionate way. Not to put too fine a point on it, it is about love.

Kindness is hardwired into our evolution as a species. As a result, kindness produces dopamine and oxytocin in our bodies — the so-called happy chemicals. Each act of kindness can also boost the immune system, increasing resistance and reducing anxiety.

Not all human beings are endowed with sufficient milk of it, making its scarcity of great importance.

Things don't always go right, particularly when you're responding to change at speed. I find being grounded in these four principles gives me resilience, and having a purpose to guide me provides a more enhanced mental fitness to cope. Challenges and setbacks can be easier to deal with if they are seen in the wider perspective of the worthwhile journey you are committed to.

So there is a lot to be said for identifying an inner excitement and commitment that will drive efforts to deliver over the long haul. Which poses the question: where will I find that meaning? A purpose that will be the source of my enthusiasm? Something that will make things happen, day in and day out?

Finding your purpose is not a race

There are many issues involved in defining a purpose. One is our natural mindset. Do we have a proactive or a reactive mindset? Do we respond to events, or do we pioneer new solutions to problems before others even perceive them? Is our locus of control internal, or do events control us?

The truth, I suspect, is messier than psychologists would have us believe. And the important thing is not to worry if you find you have no overwhelmingly meaningful point of focus for your emotional and intellectual engagement.

There is no hurry to be first past the finishing line in finding a purpose. Indeed, as we saw above, some elements of the finishing line may morph over time.

For those — like me — who are slow to alight on a focused passion, it may take not only time but many versions, diversions and a few cul-de-sacs to find it. This is normal, and should not cause concern. The important thing is to learn from the journey towards — and through the manifestations of — purpose. And not to be dispirited by the dead ends you may encounter along the way.

In simple terms, finding a purpose means finding something you enjoy. Not just doing pleasant things with pleasant people (though that can help), but trying things you feel instinctively will give you a buzz when you do them. And something that is satisfying. Satisfaction of this kind is more important than short-term happiness, which comes and goes and doesn't tend to be long-lasting. Satisfaction and fulfilment, on the other hand, tend to be more substantial. You can have setbacks, bad days or even weeks, but if you find what you are doing fulfilling, it's somehow OK, and you press ahead.

In terms of the work you do, it should — if at all possible — be aligned with your purpose. We spend so many of our waking hours working that it makes sense for work to be the start point for the journey. That's true whether you are looking for a career readjustment or replacement, or just a sizeable side income. We'll come to this in the next chapter.

There are many worthwhile issues and challenges to address. Finding the one most relevant to you at this point in your life is where to focus most energy.

And a sensible starting point to help work out what that might be, is to look at your values.

Values

To clarify, values are different from morals and principles. The latter are unchanging. My core principles of honesty, fairness, compassion and kindness don't change with circumstances. They are not relative to the situation I find myself in.

But values, by necessity, adjust to your life events.

Tidiness, for example, may be something you value, but once you have young children it may have to take a back seat for a time. Being financially well off may be important at one time in your life, but adopting the mindset of Living on Less (see Chapter 5) may see financial reward dropping way down your list of the key values to focus your life around.

Which is why agility is so important. As what you value adapts, you may need to spring nimbly to your new cause or be accepting of a new reality — while not taking leave of your core principles.

Start mapping

Understanding your values and embracing their flexibility will give you real insights into who you are at this point, who you aspire to be, and where you might look to find more meaning in your life. It is a mystery that is never quite solved, and that is part of what makes life so interesting. Just as you will change over time as life events add to the richness of your character, so too will your values change.

In order to highlight and, importantly, to prioritise your values, the first step I suggest is to create a values map.

This can take time, and considerable thinking about. Don't rush it. Here is a list of values to start with. There are likely to be values that are important to you, but are not included in the list — if so, add them.

Accountability
Ambition
Behaving morally
Being competitive
Being creative
Being liked
Belonging
Broad vision
Care for the environment
Caution
Compassion
Control
Cooperation
Courage
Creating value
Dialogue
Domain balance
    (physical, emotional,
    mental, spiritual)
Efficiency
Empathy
Enthusiasm
Fairness
Family
Flexibility
Focus
Forgiveness
Friends
Future generations
Gentleness
Harmony
Helping others
Honesty

Humour / fun
Image
    (how others see you)
Independence
Insight/understanding
Integrity
Interdependence
Kindness
Knowledge
Learning
Love
Meaning
Nutrition
Openness
Perseverance
Personal development
Physical exercise
Pride
Productivity
Respect
Responsibility
Reward
Security
Self-discipline
Self-improvement
Serving the community
Social responsibility
Status
Tradition
Trust
Wealth
Wisdom
Work / life balance

Having selected your list of values that are most relevant to you, now take time to rank them. You are aiming to get to your top ten values in order of significance that you already do, or intend to, live by. All the values on the list may seem worthwhile, but their importance, deep down, to you is what you are looking for.

The list intentionally includes my four principles of honesty, fairness, compassion and kindness. This recognises that the categories of what constitutes a value and what constitutes a principle are not rigid. Importantly, it gives you a fix on where they are now in your values hierarchy.

When you have refined your personal list to identify your top ten, you will probably find one or two of the values near the top of the list that are not getting a fair share of your focus and energy at the moment. They are important to you, and you haven't been paying enough attention to them. This will give you insight into how your life may need to change to accommodate this.

Over time, I suggest you make two lists. The first, and most important, is the list of your own values. And the other is the list of the values of your current workplace, if you have one. If there is a considerable difference between the two, which is possible, this in itself will be enlightening. It may indicate you need to relocate to a workplace more in tune with the values you want to live by.

My list of values has changed as life events have had their impact over the years. During the early years of the sports-shoe business, my top five values were:

— **Integrity**
— **Enthusiasm**
— **Creating value**
— **Humour/fun**
— **Physical exercise**

Having lost the business, got married, and then with two young children, they changed to:

— **Family**
— **Integrity**
— **Helping others**
— **Insight/understanding**
— **Creating value**

The evolution of the list in response to what was happening in my life was significant. It confirms that it's important to evaluate what really is important to you on a fairly regular basis, so you can adjust your purpose — and thus what your energy should be focused on — to make sure it is still delivering meaning and fulfilment.

Your values map is a working document and will need updating regularly, as both your thinking evolves and your life experiences impact on its balance. It's worth keeping it somewhere accessible: a written list near your desktop, in your laptop bag, or by the bed. Somewhere you can regularly check on to see if the list is still current, and you are focusing your time and enthusiasm in the right places.

Finding magnetic north

As Arctic explorers know, 'true north' is unchanging. And we can liken that to the principles that will underpin your journey wherever it might take you. True north doesn't change.

Magnetic north, however, moves over time, just as your purpose will over the years. If you think of your purpose as your magnetic north, your values map is something to work with alongside that, guiding you towards your calling at any one point in your life.

One way that may help you clarify where your magnetic north lies is to write your own obituary. Not an obituary that you would like to have written about you when you die, but one prepared by someone who knows you well and cares about you. Someone who thinks you could have done better with your life so far. The obituary should be clear-eyed. Not glossing over your failures, but clearly identifying the potential you have that is so far unrealised.

This could change your life. As it did that of Alfred Nobel. His obituary was explosive.

Nobel was born in 1833 in Stockholm, but brought up in St Petersburg, which at the time was a vibrant and cosmopolitan city. His family was wealthy. They were highly successful arms dealers. Much of their wealth derived from their invention of sea mines, used for the first time in the Crimean War. Alfred added to their wealth by inventing dynamite.

Despite being overwhelmingly used for industrial purposes, dynamite, in the wars of the later part of the nineteenth century, contributed to the deaths and injuries of countless husbands, brothers and sons around the world. And to the pain and suffering of even more civilians.

Nobel's obituary appeared in the press and stated that the man was the cause of much human misery, and his death was to be celebrated more than mourned.

Only he wasn't dead. The obituary, printed in the French press, should have been for his brother Ludwig, who *had* just died in France.

Faced with his legacy to date — the facts of which were true — Alfred devoted his remaining years to the pursuit of peace, and to his endowment of the Nobel Peace Prize as his lasting legacy.

It is doubtful writing your own legacy through the eyes of an objective person who knows you well would have quite such a dramatic effect, but it could cause an important reappraisal of where you are at this moment in time.

Principles, values and purpose

Principles, values and purpose are things we know are important, but have a tendency to place on a 'To Do Later' list. There is so much stuff going on — all urgent, sometimes important — that it is all too easy to either dabble in it, or not get round to it at all.

The fact is that it *is* important. It could change — and supercharge — your life.

Principles are timeless. They give you your grounding in what is fundamentally important to you as a human being. Values are crucially important to you at this point in your life. They really ring the bells that will help you define the purpose to focus your activity around.

Purpose gives you two things. It gives you meaning — you know and feel what you are doing is both worthwhile and right. And it gives you peace of mind. You know that even if setbacks come not as single spies, but in battalions, you will have the mental resilience to cope.

Learning points and To Do list

1. Define a values map to clarify what is most important to you.

2. Refine it regularly in the light of experience.

3. Write your obituary as a tough but fair observer to reinforce the gaps and opportunities still to be filled and resolved.

4. Define your purpose for your current lifestage.

5. Start to live it.

6. Map this against your work and, if necessary, consider trialling different forms of work, to find what gives you a real buzz.

We always overestimate the change
that will occur over the next two years
and underestimate the change that
will occur in the next ten. Don't let
yourself be lulled into inaction.

Bill Gates

4
Work

Now we've covered the groundwork for becoming and remaining open, and rooting our lives in purpose and values, we need to apply it. One of the most important areas to welcome change and stay open to developments is work.

A rapid evolution of what will constitute work in coming years has already started. The whole landscape is changing; but the need to earn money won't go away. So, if you are comfortable where you are, be aware and be ready, as you could be in for some surprises.

The future of work

Fundamental changes will take place in the nature of work in the coming decades. They will be driven by several forces. Developments in global capitalism as a system will be a major one. As will the impacts of the climate crisis (and the potential Green Industrial Revolution). Added to which is how automation and artificial intelligence will impact on how we work, and what work we do. Let's look at this in a bit more detail.

A recent piece of research by management consultants McKinsey and Co. looked into the reality of what artificial intelligence could bring. It indicated that 60 per cent of jobs could have 30 per cent of their activities replaced by adapting current technologies, but that only 5 per cent of jobs could be totally automated.

Of course, machines replacing humans has gone on since the industrial revolution. Workers in heavy industry, just like then, are likely to be hard hit in the near future, especially those who have not been given the opportunity to develop new skills. The difference today is that AI may also replace (or at least, reduce the numbers of) managers and directors, as well as shop-floor workers.

Professional jobs too are under threat. Studying law, for example, historically a safe haven for work, may have to evolve. It is estimated that already three lawyers are in training for each job available. Add to this the hundreds of would-be lawyers coming from countries like India, and the potential of artificial intelligence to replace much of the administrative work of lawyers, and a 40- or 50-year career in the law does not look like a good prospect for too many people.

And while AI has significant capacity to disrupt traditional work for humans, new technology startups are unlikely to fill the gap. A dramatic example, often cited, is that of WhatsApp. When it was bought by Facebook in 2014 for $19 billion dollars, it only had 55 employees.

Many studies into the possible evolution of work have been undertaken by global consultancies and scenario-planning organisations. The RSA (the Royal Society for Arts and Commerce) has done some pioneering work through its Future Work Centre. The Centre has laid out four possible scenarios for how work may evolve, most interestingly including the Empathy Economy. This envisages a future of responsible stewardship where tech companies self-regulate to stem concerns and create new products that work for the benefit of all. There is a link to the full article in Resources.

An ongoing concern arising from the Future Work Centre is understanding what constitutes 'Good Work'. How decent conditions and decent pay with reasonable scope for development and fulfilment will contribute to productivity growth. And what that means for government planning.

There is also exciting thinking going on in movements like the Green New Deal. Begun in the US, the GND is a proposal to address both climate change and economic inequality. It is so called because its goal is to replicate Franklin D. Roosevelt's New Deal in response to the Great Depression. It aims to define what needs to be done to reverse climate change, and marry that to new jobs and industries to reverse economic inequality. It is now a global movement, and is heartening in that it demonstrates how fresh challenges can produce new solutions to a number of apparently siloed crises.

The corporate ladder has increasingly rotten rungs

Global pressures will mean people in corporations or organisations will feel increasingly vulnerable. The pace of competition and the downsizing that often results means an increasing number will not survive the takeovers and mergers that result. Workers can see it happening. No wonder they are preparing to get their retaliation in first.

They can see that companies and organisations are beginning to perceive long-term employees as a last resort.

It is much easier to outsource services so they can be increased or decreased quickly, according to market conditions.

HR departments are finding it is more efficient (though not necessarily cheaper) to bring in skilled independent workers where appropriate. So more and more skilled workers are deciding to become independent before they are pushed. It's a two-way movement.

Multiple skills and the 'new collar' workers

Plotting a course through the new world of work will be challenging. This will be made more so by the need to develop the multiple skills that large companies are already demanding.

IBM, for example, is partnering with universities to develop curricula that span technology, science and the professions. They are developing them to fill what are now called 'new collar' — rather than white or blue collar — jobs. These jobs demand multiple training needs to cover the breadth of knowledge and skills required.

In the UK, the trend has been pioneered by the LIS — the London Interdisciplinary School. Launched in 2021 as an undergraduate degree, LIS aims to become a world leader in its field. It is hiring scholars and professionals who are polymaths. Traditional faculties of teaching dissolve, to be replaced by evolving new cross-disciplined teaching areas.

It is aimed to be highly practical, with successful entrepreneurs in areas of innovation and high tech being involved in the teaching process. This exciting project summarises the direction of travel for the new world of work: interconnected, complex, multidisciplined and innovating across boundaries.

With this direction of travel, women are likely to increasingly take the lion's share of work. They tend to score more highly on educational achievement and interpersonal skills, both of which will be needed. This demand will be there at all levels of employment, from the worthwhile but poorly paid care workers, to higher managerial and technical roles.

The income gap widens

The people training in courses like those above will, in the early stages at least, be very bright individuals. Only a few can cover such breadth academically at a high level.

These talented individuals are likely to join the high earners in such fields as technology, law, banking and consultancies (in their also evolving states). And the gap in earning power between them and the low-skilled — and the only occasionally employed — is likely to widen and further drive social inequality.

This is reflected in the independent workforce, some of whom will choose to be self-employed — some highly paid — but many of whom may be on zero-hours contracts in the gig economy, over a million of whom are already operating in it. Zero-hours contracts may be acceptable to workers who are confident of other sources of income if no work is forthcoming. But for vulnerable workers dependent on one employer for some sort of weekly income, the possibility of no work and thus no income means the balance of power is unfairly in the favour of the employer. (Some, of course, will be doing it part-time to augment their main income and to provide some autonomy.)

Precarious work

The motivations (and income streams) of this independent workforce are many. One is the strong desire to be independent (I'm in this group). Another is the inability to find a suitable job — or any job. This is compounded by the understandable resistance of many millennials (Generation Y) and Generation Z to commit to one employer — or indeed any one career — for any length of time.

They understand that it is risky to believe an employer will stay loyal to them. They also intuit that as human inputs into work evolve over time, their current skills may become irrelevant.

I have worked as an independent with multiple income streams for over 25 years. Since selling my company, and having decided I didn't want to work for anyone else, I have been regularly re-inventing myself — and loving it — generating different income streams at different times to support myself and my growing family.

My son-in-law is a more modern example of an independent, multiple income-stream worker. Leaving art college, he has variously been a builder / musician / composer / sound recordist / chef and now, having taught himself code, is a web developer. Like many others in his position, he often combines several skills in the same working week.

It is worth noting in the context of the gig economy that a growing body of research shows high levels of satisfaction and wellbeing for gig workers. This mainly stems from control of working hours and the convenience of location. Enjoying such a flexible approach to work does rely on the open mindset we've already looked at, and the lessons we've learned from neoteny.

Economic insecurity is, of course, the overarching

worry. The lack of skill development and the absence of obvious routes to career progress also cause strain. Work intensification, i.e. too much of it, and being under pressure, also seems to be a growing concern. Both of these elements of economic insecurity, interestingly, rate higher than fear of redundancy itself. Presumably this is because in the case of redundancy, there are plenty of other similar jobs out there to take the place of the one lost.

The darker side of zero-hours contracts, these inhuman, exploitative work practices, is unacceptable. Governments have yet to get a handle on this, although progress is being made in this area, often initiated by the unions and NGOs. These practices ride roughshod over the principle of fairness.

Internships to rethink your work path

The 2021 edition of the Deloitte Global Millennial Survey covering 45 countries (see Resources) shows millennials (Generation Y) and Generation Z * expressing climate change and protecting the environment as their top issues, followed by serious misgivings about discrimination and inequality. Millennials are resilient and values-driven, believing strongly that businesses should have a purpose beyond profit. As a result, they will not accept the status quo.

Their trust in the role of business has declined rapidly. In 2018, 61% said that, 'Businesses have a very/fairly positive impact on wider society'. Just three years later in 2021 that was down to 47%. Work priorities for them were employers

---

* Demographers are not in total agreement over dates, but the general consensus is for Generation Y to be the cohort born between 1980 and 1994 and Generation Z born between 1995 and 2010.

who offered both learning potential and work-life balance, as well as an inclusive and diverse working environment. However, an increasing number, given the opportunity, would quit their jobs. The 2021 survey showed 36% of millennials and 53% of Gen Z expected to leave within two years.

This growing career dissatisfaction has brought in the mid-career internship, the 'minternship' (millennial internship), as a mid-career pivot move. This is because increasing numbers of millennials are willing to become interns in their thirties to reskill in order to shift careers into other fields. Many young professionals prioritise happiness and want to have a strong sense of purpose with their jobs. Some are working on the minimum wage, but many are working for no salary at all. Despite the financial hardships, the overall response to their new working environment is hugely positive.

Get agile…

All trends point to the fact that the ability to find, or create, work / income for yourself over the next few decades will become increasingly complex and challenging.

Gigging, either as a sideline, or as a test market for a potentially major business, has benefits. The Deloitte study confirms that it is being used by millennials for both reasons.

It also has a few other benefits worth considering. A side-project loosens you up and provides independence. It can be the first step towards potential work autonomy. And trying it as a sideline allows you to road test several ideas over time, giving you a reasonable proof of concept.

It's unlikely to be easy. A lot of your time and energy will be taken up with the day job and you will need to fill evenings and weekends to get things off the ground. This will be even tougher if you have a young family. Indeed, at such a time you may either have to delay it, or work in partnership with someone less time-starved. But the long-term benefits of being able to combine good income with autonomy are huge. And they can be supercharged by the sense of satisfaction generated by aligning the project with your purpose.

Some lessons

I have been on this journey. For more than 30 years (beginning before the internet age) I have been generating my income independent of a job of any kind. And I have learned a few painful but beneficial lessons on the way.

I had to develop a new mindset to achieve it. I had been brought up to believe that having the right job was fundamentally important in life. My father had lost his father at the age of sixteen. He had to leave school immediately to provide for his mother.

It was the Depression of the 1930s. Despite this, he managed to get a job in a bank. For most of his career, he hated it. Job-switching in the 1930s was very difficult in any case, but before he was thirty, he had to go off and serve in the Second World War. Returning to civilian life, he was grateful to have a job waiting for him in the bank, so there was no chance to start a new career. As a result of his experience he was very committed to getting a good education and qualifications for his children, and helping them find sound, long-term jobs.

This upbringing meant that starting my own business already felt pretty radical, but the thought of freelancing —building an independent income stream with no employer to provide a salary and pension — required a real shift in mindset. So here are five lessons I have learned to survive and thrive in the current (and I believe future) work landscape that may help prepare your own outlook for such an adventure:

1. **Whether your project remains a side-hustle, becomes a job replacement, or leads to a totally new adventure, it's crucial to choose something you enjoy doing.** Something you find engaging and, if possible, worthwhile. There will be hours, days, even weeks when the going is challenging. If you fundamentally enjoy the essence of what you are building, it will be much easier to ride the punches and relish the good bits.

2. **Build something that is personal to you and has distinctive added value.** Long-term businesses in the internet age are no different from old-style businesses. They are built fundamentally on relationships rather than transactions. Even if they look like they are built on transactions. They become brands, and brands are built on trust. You may start out selling your goods or services on a time-spent or project-delivered basis, but do it in a way that generates customer loyalty and, if appropriate, repeat purchase. And cherish your relationships and contacts. Most of them will be a source of support and inspiration — and only too glad to help.

3. **Trust your latent creativity.** It will ensure your business model will at least look fresh, though it may not necessarily be original (there is, as they say, nothing new under the sun). Keep improving the offer. Be flexible and look for new solutions. Being agile, you

will go through several iterations before you settle on the core offer. And you may be able to see solutions and improvements that keep you ahead of any competitors trying to copy you.

4. **Try to find an offer that creates ongoing income.**
   I confess that I didn't realise it at the time, but my Think Tanks were a case in point. Members joined at different times of the year, so there was a continuous income stream across the year. If someone left with no job to go to, they could come for free to several meetings, while they lined up a new job. I have one member who has been loyal for 25 years, wearing hats as CEO of several different companies.

5. **Stay positive and be ready for setbacks** (see Chapter 8). Look at insecurity as a stimulus, not a disaster. Once you have established one repeat income stream, the rest of your time you can stay fluid, and find new clients, or revisit old ones.

You're a long time working

A final piece of advice is not to worry or rush. Being aware of the shifting trends in the world of work is a first step. It's also worth noting that changing demographics means a shift to a more agile mindset is timely.

Lynda Gratton and Andrew Scott's *The 100-Year Life* spells this out with great clarity. The traditional model of a large group of younger people funding a small group of older people in retirement is dissolving and reversing.

Japan is the extreme example. From a peak population of 127 million, with an ageing population and very small numbers being born, by 2060 it is predicted the population could be just 87 million. The results of China's historical One Child policy is likely to have a similar impact.

The flip side to this doom and gloom is that we are living longer and in reasonable health. And the truth is that old age is not expanding — middle age is. So we have to find income streams that sustain us not just in our youth and old age, but also for an extended period in our middle years.

There is significant good news in this. An increased working life span means you have time to experiment, and get it right.

Learning points and To Do list

1. Evaluate your current work. How does it fit into your longer-term view of satisfaction and revenue?

2. Look to develop an independent short-term income stream to protect you in case of job loss.

3. Spend time exploring and creating an income scheme where you can add value and benefit from emerging trends.

Rise early. Work hard. Find oil.

John Paul Getty

If you want to know what God
thinks of money, just look
at the people he gave it to.

Dorothy Parker

5
Living on Less

The idea of living a life of thrift is not a new one. Seneca the Younger was a Roman philosopher living at the time of Christ. He actually lived a fairly colourful life, but one thing he was famous for was being a Stoic, and promoting their values.

The Stoics believed in the principles of virtue, tolerance and self-control. Both Nelson Mandela (imprisoned for 27 years) and Viktor Frankl (who survived concentration camps and subsequently wrote *Man's Search for Meaning*) were heavily influenced by the principles of Stoicism.

An important element in self-control was the renunciation of material possessions. Seneca set aside several days each month to practise the philosophy. He would wear the cheapest and thinnest of clothing, eat very little food, have no pleasures, and ask himself the question, 'Is this the condition that I fear?' By acting this way he was in effect neutralising the fear of poverty and deprivation by temporarily living in that situation. And coming through the other side.

Thrift

Living a life of thrift can be uncomfortable, especially if you did not choose to renounce wealth and material possessions. It can be a shock. Whatever spin you put on it, there is still likely to be an element of victimhood involved. Events overtook you. You weren't to blame.

I know I felt this in the early days of losing my company. But I managed to snap out of it pretty soon, due to a very supportive wife and family. I now see it as a very positive period, when I rediscovered the value of things.

Thrift is about being frugal. It is not spending money needlessly, and especially not to show off one's financial situation in relation to someone else. It can be positive because, like Seneca, you are involved in a healthy engagement with a pared-back lifestyle, and are prepared for austerity if the worst were to happen. It is also positive because it makes you more empathetic to people living lives of thrift enforced by events beyond their control.

Widening financial inequality is one of the scourges of our age, and recent global economic and political developments indicate that it is likely to get worse.

It is all too easy if you are financially privileged to live in a metaphorical gated community of not having to care too much about money. You may sympathise intellectually with the plight of those living outside the gates, but in reality money has lost its meaning for you. You may bristle at that but, unlike those who are struggling financially, I wonder if you know to the nearest pound, let alone penny, how much is in your pocket, purse or bank account.

Being open-minded and adjusting your life to one more centred on thrift puts you, to a small degree, back in touch with those struggling in a world of relentless social security cuts and living on the margins of society.

The benefit of thrift in today's work environment

The benefits of thrift are many, but the nub of the matter is that it reduces fear. It reduces fear for two reasons. Firstly, because by spending less now you could build up a little in savings. You'll then be in better shape to cope if you suddenly find your income dries up because your job no longer exists. It also allows for the inevitable dry spells involved in developing an independent income.

Secondly, it reduces fear because whatever happens in your work — the arrival of a ghastly new boss, a radical and alien change in working conditions brought about by AI — you still have choices. To a degree you retain a modicum of autonomy. You can make the choice to take voluntary redundancy or resign because you are pretty confident you will survive.

Many people in many industries have been tossed out of work when they were not prepared for it, and survived. And you will be in a better position than most because you will already be conditioned for a pared-back living situation.

It's also worth reminding yourself of something we all know in theory: in living frugally you'd appreciate that the important things in life have no financial value. You know the list: love, friendship, humour, nature, music, and so on.

All these elements — from love through to nature — constitute our wealth. The cars and the foreign holidays are fine, but they are peripheral to our fundamental wealth. Their loss would be inconvenient, and might temporarily reduce our self-image, but if we were to lose them, we would still be wealthy in real terms. Of course, this is very different from living in enforced poverty.

The difference lies in your being *in control* of your frugality, rather than it being enforced on you by an inability to generate enough income to cover more than the barest of basics.

As we saw in the previous chapter, the world of work is changing and even if you are in one of the conventionally highly paid jobs, things will be less certain in the coming decades. And beyond that, retirement ages will probably by necessity be put back to your seventies and beyond.

Building up savings in times of relative feast is the first action to take when rethinking and planning our potential future income requirements. The challenge, of course, is that whatever we are earning at the present time, we tend to spend a little more than that. And it may be that you are genuinely not earning enough to be able to put money aside right now. But just imagine you have lost your job and have no income at all, apart from the social-security safety net. That might be incentive enough to save something now, in case of even tougher times ahead.

Staying grounded

The principles of the Stoic philosophers are timeless. No wonder they were taken up by Mandela and Frankl. Both had undergone great suffering and deprivation. Both had great humanity. And both emerged stronger and more convinced of how right the principles of virtue, tolerance and self-control were to civilised living.

They remind us that life is about more than getting and spending. Their lives and teachings confirm that within all the challenges and complexities facing us today a strong moral code is as relevant now as it was to them in the twentieth century, or Seneca 2,000 years ago.

Honesty, compassion, fairness and kindness — plus mental resilience (self-control) — all provide the same broad principles the Stoics embraced.

Thrift — living on less — underpins the element of self-control, lived by the Stoics. Coupled with our strong moral code, and a worthwhile purpose, it provides a sound foundation for our work. Surfer and film-maker Mickey Smith hit the target in his Do Lecture in 2011: 'If I can only scrape a living, at least it's a living worth scraping.'

Lastly, it's worth noting that if you do lose your job, almost everyone I know or have met who has lost theirs has always said that in the long run it was the best thing that ever happened to them.

Learning points and To Do list

1. Start saving now, despite the possible discomfort. Consider eating out less, fewer holidays, saying no to overseas hen and stag do's (say 'I'm doing a Seneca!').

2. See if you can cut back on your monthly grocery bill. Divide the month into four weeks. In the first week try and cut spending by 30%, in the second by 20%, and in the final fortnight relax the cut backs.

3. Once this has been achieved, see if you can maintain the reduced rate of 20%.

4. Work out what you have saved and split the savings (50/50 or 70/30 — you decide). One chunk goes into a savings account and the other for a charity of your choice. Your empathy for the people benefitting from the charity's work is likely to have increased.

The illiterate of the 21st century will not be those who cannot read and write, but those who cannot learn, unlearn and relearn.

—

Alvin Toffler

6
Continuous Learning

The challenge and the opportunity are the same: to understand at a profound level that learning doesn't stop. And it's not just about absorbing knowledge, but questioning it.

People have talked for some time about Lifelong Learning. But it is now a simple necessity. In today's fast-paced world, we either stay agile, and relevant, or we become immobile and irrelevant.

Learning is the core resource for our futureproofing. Without understanding the past and the present, we cannot hope to understand — or prepare for — the future.

What kind of learning?

There is a debate under way about what sort of education is relevant to the 21st century, and what is the best way to learn and to grow. Should children be taught facts — which are readily available on Google — or should they be stimulated in ways that teach them to think for themselves and to be more creative in both problem-solving and developing new possibilities?

Obviously facts are vital. Knowing how the human body works is vital to a doctor. But creativity is required to find new techniques to cure disease. As well as creativity, empathy is important — having an understanding of and emotional engagement with the feelings of people who are ill. And to be a good surgeon, manual skills are vital. So wide knowledge, creativity, emotional empathy and manual skills are all learnings a surgeon requires to be effective in his or her work.

As we saw in Chapter 4, the same is true for great swathes of work in the increasing complexity of the 21st century. New knowledge, new skills and new levels of creativity will be required. So learning, in its widest — and traditional — sense, will need to cover all these areas.

Self-debating while learning

But a more relevant type of learning is also required. Not just absorbing wider knowledge and insights, but also the mindset to challenge sources of information. Critically assessing ideas and self-debate while learning have become more important. The best universities have always taught students to question everything. Lectures and supervisions are intended to make students question received wisdom, not to supply lecture notes for use in an exam.

This applies to all wisdom. Social philosopher Charles Handy has put it this way:

You cannot be a good academic unless you are willing to question the accepted wisdom, even to believe that you yourself might be wrong. To question your own beliefs and actions is often the best way of learning.

This applies to the past and the present but also the future. The accepted wisdom Handy alludes to is made up of a combination of history and the present day. The insights and learnings that make up what we take as accepted wisdom today may also contain a widely held view on what the future might look like. His point is that we need to question all those perceptions.

Accepted wisdom is likely to be the product of fixed mindsets. The wisdom needs to be questioned, because an open mindset may join dots — from the past, the present or the future — and see connections that render it invalid.

Agile learning

Agile learning is a developing approach to both the selection and training of workers in future-focused organisations. But this approach is relevant to all areas of activity — be they social, or related to work. It is defined as the ability to quickly and continuously learn and unlearn mental models and practices from a variety of sources.

Put simply, it means learning by doing, iterating and improving as you go. Agile learning has been ramped up as a desirable skill for organisations — and for life in general — by the rapid evolution of job roles. As we saw in Chapter 4, these new roles often require a wider base of skills (the ability to be something of a polymath) and, critically, the ability to unlearn skills that have become obsolete.

A growth mindset is important, because letting skills go can be the difficult bit. Being agile enough to let them go is as critical to being future-ready as being open to new ideas when they first emerge.

This flexibility is becoming one of the critical factors in the potential for someone to flourish in today's — and tomorrow's — world. Mentally agile workers will be very adaptive to change, and will be able to tackle new problems and situations with ease.

Critically, agile learning as a recognised and approved way of operating legitimises failure in a more systemic way. Failure officially becomes a part of learning. It always has been, but this gives it a further seal of approval. In the words of Matthew Taylor, former chief executive of the RSA: 'Institutions need to be experimental, agile and adaptive, as able to learn from failure as scale up success.'

The significance of agile learning is evidenced by the fact that the top leadership and talent management consultancies include it in assessing candidates. They analyse an employee's potential by two criteria. First, by the conventional ability to learn — the essential cognitive ability to absorb knowledge and identify patterns, trends and logical rules in data.

They then apply a second criterion: the future-focused analysis of what is termed the orientation to learn. Orientation to learn is not only having the basic behavioural competencies to learn new things, but to update and adapt them faster. Put another way: to be open-minded.

A practical definition of the concept, and advice on how to develop more agility in learning, comes from William Montgomery, founder and CEO of TEN Ltd, a highly regarded management and talent development consultancy in the UK. He states:

> **Research has found that learning agility — the ability to grow and use new strategies — is a good indicator of whether someone can be a high performer. Learning-agile employees are able to jettison skills and ideas that are no longer relevant. And learn new ones that are.**

He then supplies five very practical behaviours, based in the real-world experience of his clients, that will cultivate learning agility. Broadly speaking, they are as follows:

Ways to develop agile learning

1. **When faced with new and complex situations, look first for similarities to past projects.** Before jumping to conclusions, listen deeply, in order to fully understand. Clear the mind before reacting, and practise calming techniques, like deep breathing. This recognises the reality that in challenging situations, the pressure of events can temporarily immobilise the brain.

2. **Innovating.** Seeking out new solutions and repeatedly asking yourself, 'What else?'

3. **Seek out input from others.** Ask colleagues and friends for suggestions on how it could have been done better. Open-minded reflection on their — and your — inputs and reactions after the event can free up new and better solutions.

4. **Gain experience by actively seeking out 'stretch' assignments where success isn't a given.** This means challenging yourself regularly in a positive way to make sure your learning doesn't slip back into the comfort zone of a closed mind.

5. **Never defend action taken.** Always acknowledge failures and capture the lessons learned.

Put another way, genuine learning means being open minded.

Learning for pleasure and developing new skills

> Every time I learn something new,
> it pushes old stuff out of my brain.

Homer Simpson

Learning is satisfying. And can also be fun. Homer Simpson may not be directly educational, but he is certainly amusing. And, as with most well-written comedy, he not only makes us laugh, but also provides moments of penetrating insight. We often feel our learning capability is finite. But in fact it is infinitely elastic. We all know people who are still learning into advanced age. I know I am. For work, and for life in general, learning is, and should be, interesting, enjoyable — and continuous.

I was lucky enough to study English Literature at university. Now, decades later, I go to a weekly evening class run by a brilliant teacher at a local school. It is a joy. I relish both learning new insights and developing a deeper appreciation of poets and novelists I am already familiar with, and discovering new ones. It is even more satisfying when I am introduced to writers that I thought I didn't like, but on closer acquaintance have come to value enormously.

So it is important to look at learning and relearning not as a chore but as an enriching challenge. To see it as an opportunity to rethink and refresh. A positive, open approach to learning will give you the chance to escape frozen thinking. Thinking becomes frozen when you have unconsciously remained in a comfort zone of groupthink that has failed to acknowledge that the world has moved on in a specific area of sensibility. You are out of kilter with current reality, and need to update your attitude or perspective on the issue.

Agile learning will refresh and invigorate your mind. It will move your brain from a state of immobility to mobility. And, importantly, your positive, engaged approach will make your learning stimulating and fun.

Developing soft skills

Learning in its widest sense will also include the development of new skills, in particular your soft skills. Their development is as important as improving technical expertise, or personal interest.

Key to this is your ability to initiate and develop personal relationships. Your personal networks, which will be crucial to your long-term surviving and thriving, will mean you are paying conscious attention to honing relationships. They may be built online, without your ever meeting someone in person. But there is a human connection nonetheless. You build the crucial element of any relationship through trust. And trust is built by trustworthy behaviour.

That said, the fact is that you can't beat a face-to-face meeting to develop a relationship. There is a good reason the events industry is vast and growing. People like meeting and spending time with other people. Organisations find that human interaction is the most effective way to build culture and coherence. The millions spent on team-building exercises are, for the most part, spent for a good reason. They work.

So do take any opportunity to go to conferences, and go on courses and workshops. You will be able to learn new information, but almost as important, to question it and debate it with the people you meet. Your wide base of learning — and questioning — will mean it will be stimulating for you ... and for them.

It will also give you the opportunity to initiate and develop your soft skills, as you meet new people from varied backgrounds. Developing relationships with a wide range of people will both keep you open and increase your knowledge and insights.

Being prepared

> Time spent in reconnaissance
> is seldom wasted.
>
> Attributed to Sun Tzu

As we touched on in Chapter 4, a lot of thinking and resource is going into helping people prepare for the coming changes.

Even if you don't have a corporate job, it's important to be aware of developments — for both your work and life skills. Corporations and governments are hard at work pioneering and cooperating in new learning and training initiatives. And some are worth knowing about.

In the area of learning development, one potentially important initiative is the so-called personal training accounts — providing every worker, both employed and self-employed, with funds to reskill and/or improve their knowledge base. These schemes are already being piloted by the governments of France and Singapore.

The more enlightened planners are also thinking in terms of developing upskilling programmes for all levels of workers — including those on the shop floor. Such programmes would aim to help them improve their high-touch customer-service skills and their capacity to interact with new technologies like robotics.

It is also happening independently, from the grass roots up. In the US, the campaign group OUR Walmart, a union-associated group, has launched the WorkIt app. It leverages AI to supercharge the expertise of trained advisors and gives information on workplace rights. Already, as a result, over half a million employees have received a significant increase in paid family leave.

From another angle, a dramatic pioneer is Pursuit, based in New York. By training low-income workers to upskill in computer programming, it has raised their incomes from $18,000 to $85,000 on average.

Where to learn?

MOOCs — Massive Open Online Courses — are an opportunity to learn at low cost and are potentially a superb resource for gaining new knowledge and skills or upgrading old ones. It is very much an idea whose time has come, and could not be more relevant to the educational development needs of countless individuals in the years ahead.

The Open University in the UK, of course, has been pioneering the concept in paid form for decades. It has now been joined by courses run at a global scale put together in the main by European, US and Chinese universities.

The variety is immense, from Data Analysis to an Introduction to Functional Programming, Cash Flow in Startups and an Introduction to Robotics.

A wide choice in the humanities is also included offering broader, deeper learning. The richness and breadth of business learning is demonstrated by courses focused on building social or not-for-profit organisations.

The price range for MOOCs is as massive as their title. From good courses for £20 or less, to fully certified degrees, with their concomitant costs. So check the small print before signing up. The top business schools are now seriously engaged, but do make sure the course you might be interested in remains free throughout the programme. A good place to start is *mooc-list.com*, but look at other websites too.

Remember TED talks and The Do Lectures

Access to information and insights into life skills (although possibly living skills is a better description) is, of course, readily available. The Do Lectures, TED Talks, RSA Lectures, The School of Life, the list is endless. Insightful talks abound on psychology, the workings of the human brain, love, shame, politics, culture. You name it, it's all there. Each talk (usually about twenty minutes or less) supplies a rich store of easily accessible wisdom and information. It is easier than in any time in history to take over the management of your own education and career(s) development. The investment, as with MOOCs, is in your time rather than your money. The richness of fare available would make it an act of almost gross stupidity not to make the investment.

Energy management

Part of learning is about energy management, rather than time management. Are you a morning person or an evening person? This is important, because it makes a significant impact on your ability to absorb, process and remember information.

Learning obviously takes place all the time, but formalised learning, like a MOOC or actively listening to a lecture or podcast, might be much more effective for you early in the morning before work, or much later in the evening. Experiment to see what works well for you.

Getting out and learning from people you know

It's all too easy to just do things online, on the commute, on the sofa. But 9 times out of 10, physically going to a talk or workshop will produce the serendipitous nuggets you can't get otherwise. As I mentioned above, there are significant benefits in attending conferences. Not only do you learn about new trends and ideas, but importantly, meet people where mutually beneficial relationships can start.

Networking groups — formal and informal — are worth considering. I have a film producer friend who is a member of a large and longstanding networking group for people in the industry. Made up of producers, actors, financiers, directors and writers, it is over two thousand strong, and a limit of two hundred members meet four times a year. There is no membership fee, you just chip in for any costs on the night. Have a look for one in your industry, and if one doesn't exist, consider forming one of your own.

The objective of such a group for you would be simple: to find new ideas — ideas that would both deliver your purpose and, possibly, create income. These ideas might come quickly, or they may provide seedcorn to your subconscious that takes years to grow. But it is all good fodder to keep your brain active, agile and open to new possibilities.

And, of course, to help your fellow members enjoy the same benefits.

Make a note

Capturing ideas from any source when they emerge is important, for they have a tendency to slip away and be lost forever. You think you'll remember, but you won't. Carry a small notebook to jot down ideas, have a sheet of paper by the bed, or add a note on your phone. Some ideas I cannot for the life of me decipher in the morning, but most get through in some form or another.

Learning is about more than enhancing the work you do

What we are talking about is personal growth. It is about stimulation. Because being interested makes you interesting. However large a time sponge your work may become in your life, it is worth hanging on to the truth that you are more than your work. As we will see in the next chapter, you are defined by your overall contribution to life.

That contribution will be dramatically enhanced by embracing learning agility. As we know, there are many things competing for our time. So getting good at prioritising what is relevant to you in learning makes sense. Learning is about three things:

1. **Absorbing the right information** from as wide a number of sources as possible.

2. **Processing that information** — joining up both the obvious and the unexpected dots — so it provides an informed and relevant basis on which to take action.

3. **Providing stimulation**, so you are positively and enthusiastically engaged in developing both your work and your life in general.

Life is never easy. To know what information is the right information, you need to do some wide learning in the first place to make sure you can develop an accurate perspective of hindsight and foresight. This will include both your own country's history, as well as that of foreign countries (especially countries of growing global importance, like China or India); plus watching factual documentaries, and reading widely on social and business trends.

You need to understand the mistakes and the successes of the past, and have an informed view on the exciting potential of the future. Once your basic learning has been undertaken, you need to stay informed and up to date, and continuously evaluate your perspective of the priorities and possibilities of the future.

This well-informed perspective is important, because agile learning is far more effective if the agility stimulated is based on wide knowledge and informed insight. So agile learning is not just about absorbing information, but being able to process it to distinguish between the relevant and the irrelevant. Then to be able to respond with confidence, accuracy and speed.

And in doing so, to develop a significant level of futureproofing.

Learning points and To Do list

1. Establish the best time of day for you to read effectively — for absorption and retention. Aim to rapidly reprise ideas learnt (first or last thing of the day). Repetition reinforces learning.

2. Read widely and be curious about lots of areas. There's truth in the saying, 'Readers are Leaders'.

3. Make sure you cover the waterfront: be aware of trends and happenings in society, politics, and the arts. Track trends in business, technology, and the media.

4. Listen frequently to talks on psychology, social trends, plus areas of personal interest.

5. Write things down! You won't remember everything. And regularly review what you've written. It's a wasted asset if it's left unviewed in your phone or notebook.

**Live as if you were to die tomorrow.
Learn as if you were to live forever.**

Mahatma Gandhi

Gratitude exists because the gift is not paid for. Any reward cuts off the force of gratitude.

Lewis Hyde, *The Gift*

7
Giving Back

Evolution has hardwired us to help each other for the simple reason that helping each other is beneficial to human survival. And as social beings it also creates and maintains social bonds.

Kindness, generosity and altruism are rewarded with feel-good endorphins. Not only are these mood enhancers valuable and enjoyable in their own right, but they are also effective in counteracting the stress hormones of cortisol and adrenaline. And as we've already seen in Chapter 1, it can be harder to move into a growth mindset if we're dealing with stress. So let's look at how getting our thinking — and our emotions — into a context that is other-orientated can have a positive impact on our own state of mind, as well as being worthwhile in its own right.

Everything we have covered so far — from the way you rethink work, to finding purpose, and living on less — is underpinned by the principles that ground us. In my case, fairness, compassion, honesty and, of course, kindness. Giving back really brings each of these into focus.

Fairness, because your relative wealth — in terms of money, wellbeing and ability to articulate on behalf of others — is likely to be in excess of the person or cause you are helping or supporting. Whether it's climate change or those suffering from mental illness, you are in a privileged position. You can support the homeless, for example, because you know you're where you are through a significant degree of luck (education, inherited brainpower, family background, connections, self-confidence) as much as merit. And, similarly, those you are helping may not be there through idleness or lack of merit. Many will have a strong work ethic but lack the privileges you may have had, including luck.

Compassion, because you feel for the deprivation, suffering, bad luck or despair of those you are helping.

Honesty, because deep down you know your lot in life is a relatively privileged one, and you can spare time and effort (or simply some loose change) to help people less privileged.

Kindness, because your heart naturally goes out to people who are suffering or in need.

The essence of giving

Giving, to be worthy of the name, expects no rewards.

Seneca also understood giving. 'There is no grace,' he said, 'in a benefit [i.e. gift] that sticks to the fingers.' If you are expecting something in return — however implicitly stated, or however far in the future — that isn't a gift. It's either a deal or a bribe.

To give — whether it is time, expertise, money, or just your compassionate presence — has to be wholehearted, and with no strings attached.

This fact is one of the many insights of Adam Smith, the great eighteenth-century Scottish philosopher. Smith was given the title of the Father of Economics. His ideas today seem strikingly modern. The concept of the division of labour, of human capital and the invisible hand were all his. He also had the following profound insight relevant to our times: 'No society can surely be flourishing and happy, of which the far greater part of the members are poor and miserable.'

On giving, he was similarly perceptive:

How selfish soever man may be supposed, there are evidently some principles in his nature which interest him in the fortunes of others, and render their happiness necessary to him, though he derives nothing from it except the pleasure of seeing it. … The greatest ruffian, the hardest violator of the rules of society, is not altogether without it.

This is an early insight into what is now called the Helper's High. This concept came into focus in the 1980s, and has been confirmed by several studies since then. It describes the uplifting feeling you get after doing a good deed or act of kindness. As Smith pointed out, it is rooted in our natural instincts to help fellow human beings.

There are several forms of giving, of course, but the one I find most rewarding is volunteering. From personal experience, I can vouch for the existence and efficacy of the Helper's High. For more than twenty years, I volunteered at Wandsworth Prison or at Wormwood Scrubs to visit, and subsequently mentor, inmates, most of whom were only months away from their release date. Even those who were far from being released, and had committed serious crimes, were engaging, and I always left feeling better for the visit.

There are several reasons for this. The underlying one was the profound feeling of 'There but for the grace of

God, go I.' Some of the back-stories were truly horrendous. Many could neither read nor write and came from very broken, and often very violent, homes. They were often drug-dependent, many had mental health challenges and had associated throughout their lives with similar people who'd had few chances to make any sort of progress in life.

What really motivated me to go through the lengthy process of getting through security, waiting while door after door was unlocked, was that I had the sense — in most cases — that they were worthwhile human beings. They just wanted a chance to sort their lives out. The first few visits were always about building up trust. This has meant gently probing their story as to why they were there, in prison.

At the first meeting, they usually claim total innocence of any crime. But after a few sessions many come to admit their guilt. A positive relationship has invariably built up, and this has been cemented if they were released, and I've been able to help them through the very challenging process of walking out of prison, back into a world that looked strange and unwelcoming. I still see one of the prisoners I mentored back in 2017 (he was on Britain's Most Wanted list at the time of his arrest) for a coffee every month or so. Talking to other volunteers who visit and mentor prisoners, we all look forward to our visits, and share a real buzz from the work.

Qualification for helper's high

If you are giving in the form of volunteering, you need to be genuine in your motivation. If you are doing it to impress other people, it will be like the gift that sticks to your fingers. An ulterior motive is involved. And most people — including yourself — won't be fooled.

This was brought home to me when I was on a very interesting and effective training course in my early days as a prison mentor. The course began with us being asked to mix rapidly with our classmates and chat to them for a short period of time.

We were then asked by the leader to sit in the centre of a circle, one by one, while our new classmates around us shared their impressions of who we were. It was astounding. We were all, myself included, given an impression of ourselves that was eye-openingly accurate. As the leader said, people — prisoners especially — can smell who you are. And in particular they can smell whether you have integrity.

Be genuine in your giving

While I now know the Helper's High works, initially I had no idea of its existence. Beyond a general feeling of fulfilment, there are multiple other benefits that most volunteers — like myself — are only dimly aware of, but confirm a general feeling that the experience, though often challenging, is worthwhile. And you want to go back for more. Multiple studies have shown that the beneficial effects of volunteering are both physical and mental:

1. **Volunteering lowers blood pressure.** A study from Carnegie University produced evidence that adults over the age of fifty who volunteered regularly were less likely to develop high blood pressure. It also increased their level of physical activity.

2. **It reduces stress.** Part of the Helper's High is the release of oxytocin, which is a chemical that boosts

our mood. It also counteracts the effects of cortisol, which induces the feeling of stress. Not only that, it can create a virtuous loop. The higher the level of oxytocin, the more you want to help others. That in turn stimulates the creation of serotonin and dopamine, the 'happiness' chemicals.

3. **It increases self-esteem.** A Cornell University study showed that levels of self-esteem were increased by volunteering, through a feeling of greater mastery of life (it also pointed to increased levels of energy).

4. **It enhances the immune system.** Studies have shown that the positive feelings resulting from volunteering increase the body's number of T-cells — the cells that help the body both resist disease and recover more quickly when you have been ill. Indeed, it is an effective defence against flu and the common cold.

5. **It reduces depression and loneliness, and encourages greater social cohesion.** Because volunteering tends to be a hands-on interaction with other human beings — often in a less fortunate position than yourself — it can be an effective antidote for depression. At the same time it can reduce loneliness — both for the volunteer and for the person being helped.

There are numerous other benefits claimed for volunteering — from weight loss to increasing your trust level, which all point towards a sixth benefit: A longer and healthier life. A study of three thousand volunteers over an almost ten-year period showed lower death rates and a higher incidence of good health than those who did not volunteer. In addition, a study at the University of Buffalo concluded that 'helping others reduced mortality, specifically by buffering the association between stress and mortality'.

The act of helping others can provide purpose, while also being a motivator to you to change your perspective — it opens minds. The great good fortune of this situation is that the benefits once again point in both directions. While the receivers are obviously the primary beneficiaries, the givers receive significant benefits as well.

Other types of giving

There are, of course, many kinds of giving, beyond volunteering. In today's time-starved world, giving time — such as helping with neighbours, young children, a sick friend or relative — is one of the most generous. Indeed, if you are time poor, it is one of the biggest gifts you can give.

It can be even more rewarding for all concerned if you can combine your natural talents and skills within the gift. Like using DIY skills to solve problems for someone who is incapacitated, or your patience and IT skills to reduce the frustrations of an older relative.

The thing to remember is that you have many gifts to give. You may not think you do, but you have many skills that countless people could benefit from (theatricals, singing, painting, gardening, entertaining children, your wisdom, mobility, sympathy, energy, trust, friendship, support, your love).

A possibly unexpected gift that is yours to give more frequently than perhaps you do now, is recognition. David Dunn wrote a book published a hundred years or so ago called *Try Giving Yourself Away*. It is of its time — folksy, to say the least — but it remains a gem. It is about different types of giving, but it centres on recognition.

From winning an Oscar to a pat on the back, or being told you are doing a good job, is uplifting and motivating. Recognising people for their achievements in all walks of life is something everyone responds to. Who doesn't feel good when made to feel appreciated?

Feeling valued is a basic human need. From health professionals to hospital cleaners, from senior managers to just-joined trainees, if someone feels valued, they will not only work more wholeheartedly, they will go the extra mile. So obvious, yet so ignored.

One proviso. David Dunn is very clear that the praise must be strictly genuine. As with gifts not sticking to fingers, praise must be honest, and not looking for any reward. In his words, 'today's giveaway is a blind investment in future happiness'.

Another proviso. In the wider field of giving — especially of time — don't be too profligate. Sometimes, when asked for help, the appropriate answer is to politely say no. As a busy person, you are likely to be asked to do things that you simply don't have the time to deliver effectively.

Your contribution is bigger than what you give

Giving is great, and it's important. But contribution is a bigger and richer concept. It is about creating a living legacy.

Your living legacy is the positive mark you are currently making on your family, your friends, your work and your community or society overall. Your wider contribution has always been important, but its significance has increased in recent years. This is because, as a society, our priorities have changed. Work may take up a lot of our waking hours and attention, but its importance to us has diminished.

Taking the UK figures from the World Values Survey, and the Trajectory Global Foresight Study, the following important and surprising trend emerges: work is becoming less important to us.

How important is the following in your life?		
	1999	2018
Work	49%	24%

This is an extraordinary shift. It means our free, or leisure, time now trumps work in its importance in our lives. This obviously includes the so-called experience economy (travel, eating out, entertainment), but the reduction of work as an overriding priority means there has been an important realignment of our priorities.

Underlying the relevance of your contribution is the growing desire — validated by much research — to make a difference. Your contribution may be large — you may make a discovery that counteracts global warming. Or it may be on a smaller scale — being a nourishing and supportive parent. Whatever scale it is, it will be your living legacy.

The many variations on the Helper's High will both sustain and inspire you as you move through life, and your legacy evolves. You will be confident you are leaving a positive footprint.

Not only that, it is a manifestation of your essential humanity. Your kindness and generosity means your giving mindset will not be selfish or self-indulgent because it has strong foundations. Because you are grounded, your contribution will be worthwhile.

Learning points and To Do list

1. Look for opportunities to be kind and compassionate. To relatives and friends, but also to people you come across during the day. Look out for people in need (try asking), especially the elderly and parents with very young children, as they are likely to need it more than most.

2. Find a cause that resonates with you, and volunteer to help in some specific, regular way. It can be for a local, national or international cause or charity, but find one where your emotional engagement gets deeper, the more active you are. If that doesn't happen, experiment till you find a cause that truly engages your heart.

3. Be conscious of, and enjoy, a Helper's High. You've earned it!

4. Congratulate people on merit and contribution whenever possible. But be genuine.

5. From these actions, develop a giving mindset that underlies your whole being. Keep giving, until it becomes part of who you are.

**The applause of a single human being
is of great consequence.**

Dr Samuel Johnson

Everything can be taken away from
a man but one last thing: the last of the
human freedoms: to choose one's own
attitude in any set of circumstances,
to choose one's own way.

Viktor Frankl, *Man's Search for Meaning*

8
Attitude

Viktor Frankl was transported to the Auschwitz death camp, where he lost friends and family, including his wife, who was pregnant with their child at the time. He resisted the overwhelming temptation to surrender to his circumstances.

His book, *Man's Search for Meaning*, was written after his release, when he was working as a practising psychiatrist. It summarises how he retained a positive outlook, giving him resilience, which in turn allowed him to retain his sense of autonomy.

This chapter is a summary of my learnings on the importance of a positive attitude, and how to develop and retain one. Let's start with a challenge.

The 24-hour challenge

The 24-Hour Challenge is simple but not easy.

To take it, you must commit to not saying anything negative about anyone or anything, to anyone, for 24 hours. This means no tittle-tattle, no passing on of rumours, no speaking badly of people, however much they deserve it.

No eyes rolling when someone has done something particularly stupid. No nodding when someone else is speaking ill of a person you know. Or even don't know.

You get the message. No negatives about anything or anyone. And walk away when negativity is happening around you.

You are pretty unlikely to last for 24 hours. If you do, well done. If you don't, start the 24 hours again. And keep starting it again until you can do the full 24-hour period.

Then move to a week. Then go for a month without being, or implying, anything negative about anyone. Once you can do this, you'll find it comes as second nature not to listen to, or pass on, negative comments about anyone.

I did this some years ago. I still have the occasional lapse but the interesting thing is that if I do, I start to blush, and feel bad about it. Overall, avoiding the negative, and confirming what is positive, is genuinely life-enhancing and helps to keep a positive outlook. Developing such a positive mental attitude is fundamental to ensure the thinking in this book comes alive. It will deliver the intended benefits of mental agility, being attuned to the future, and being committed to uplifting principles. Without the energy and excitement generated by an enthusiastic approach to life, entropy follows.

Entropy is the second law of thermodynamics. It identifies the tendency of the universe to slide towards disorder. Without energy, and effort, things decay. In the words of Steven Pinker, best-selling author and Professor of Cognitive Psychology at Harvard:

The ultimate purpose of life, mind, and human striving: to deploy energy and information to fight back the tide of entropy and carve out refuges of beneficial order.

We are not looking for refuges, but we are looking to develop a mindset that is open, resilient and positive. Positivity is the starting point of all three.

My learnings

Many books have been published on attitude and positive thinking. Over the past two or three decades I have read a lot of them. Some are excellent. Some less so. But they all contain nuggets of insight that are worth taking on board.

Here are seven ideas that have worked best for me — I've included a couple that I've come across on my life's journey that have also been effective. Here we go.

1. Avoid miserabilism

Reading newspapers, websites or listening to podcasts that are miserabilist in nature is a sure route to feeling miserable yourself. Just watching the news on TV can sometimes fall into this category.

A lot of bad stuff goes on in the world, but wallowing in it doesn't help. As we saw earlier, pessimism and depressive thinking are disabling. The result is learned helplessness. Nothing is worth doing, so nothing gets done. So filter your intake of media carefully. Stay open, and just collect enough information to keep you well informed on what is going on in the world, but don't overdose. Avoid the extreme examples of miserabilist media.

2. Avoid toxic people

Birds of a feather flock together. This truth about the power of association has been validated by countless studies.

Smokers tend to associate with smokers, overweight people tend to associate with overweight people, and so on. It is understandable — there is safety in numbers.

As we saw in the opening chapter, this is a difficult one, because it can also relate to friends and family. But the power of association is particularly strong with people close to you who are negative. Distance needs to be created, however challenging it may be in the short term, to avoid the effects of toxicity. And as a result, you will have to understand that you need to work harder to avoid being disabled by the negative.

The positive-thinking industry has a word for toxic people: drains. They suck the energy and the life out of you. Positive people, on the other hand, are called radiators. They provide heat and warmth. I know where I'd prefer to stand.

3. Feel good about yourself

To be a radiator, rather than a drain, you need to feel good about yourself. It seems obvious, but radiating positivity and encouragement comes from an inner core of self-esteem that uplifts not only you, but the people around you.

In one of the classic self-help books by David Schwartz called *The Magic of Thinking Big*, he suggests that each time you meet, or talk to someone, ask yourself the question, 'Does that person honestly feel better because they talked to me?'

And one important extra benefit radiators have in reinforcing people's self-belief is helping to avoid any feeling of victimhood. This is the insidious feeling of being a victim constantly put-upon by life, and powerless to fight the alien forces set against you. Why do negative things always happen to me? Why am I always unlucky? Why don't I get the breaks?

The reason you don't get the breaks is that feeling sorry for yourself is deeply unattractive. People are not keen to help you. That's why it's important to be a radiator. Radiators exude positive energy and enthusiasm. Drains suck the air and the feeling of wellbeing out of a room.

4. Have the Golden Key handy

The Golden Key is a mental resilience reinforcing technique that most of us could do with at one time or another. I learned the concept from Marcus Child, a brilliant inspirer and communicator of the benefits of positivity and work / life balance (see Resources).

It's for those really tough days when you arrive home shattered. All you want is to sink into a chair and recover in your own time. Instead, you reach into your bag or pocket. At this point your front door key becomes golden. The transmuted key transforms you into an enthusiastic, energetic and doting partner, parent, friend or relative, who is genuinely delighted to see all those within. Enter smiling.

It works.

5. Look for the good

There are two concepts involved here — both bearing the same name.

The first takes some adjusting to, but I have always found it helpful. The concept is simple: good always comes from bad, eventually. When something bad happens, at some point, somewhere, good will come from it. If you don't get a deserved promotion, then a more suitable and more interesting work opportunity will appear later. Sometimes you have to wait to see the good and appreciate it. And it is a useful counterbalance to self-pity.

The second concept is that whatever happens around us, we tend to focus on the negative, and ignore the good. This is a validated psychological condition that stems from our evolution as a species. When we were being hunted by competitive life forms hungry for a meal, we developed the capacity to screen out positive things within our environment, and only concentrated on threats. Traces of that embodied mindset remain, in our tendency to look for the bad things that happen around us, ignoring the good. In fact, it is said that it takes five positive things to have the same impact as one single negative thing.

6. Look after yourself

Healthy living is an enabler and supercharges a positive mindset. All of the basics are important. So don't neglect any of them.

Sleep

A minimum of seven hours — deep, if possible.

If you're stressed, and sleep is difficult, try some breathing exercises — see the excellent *Do Breathe* by Michael Townsend Williams. What I've also found very helpful is the advice I heard from a lecture given by Deepak Chopra many years ago. A world-renowned pioneer in personal development and Clinical Professor of Medicine, his message was simple: if you can't sleep, instead of worrying and letting your inability to sleep keep you awake for longer, just lie on your back or your side. Breathe calmly, and relax totally. The benefits of this are almost the same as actually being asleep. So when morning comes, you'll be as refreshed as if you had slept all night. The five-minute YouTube clip in Resources gives more detail.

Exercise

Mens sana in corpore sano. The Latin tag, meaning 'a healthy mind in a healthy body', has always had a ring of truth, but it is now validated by countless studies around the world. Exercise is now recommended by health bodies and governments for its ability to improve mental, as well as physical, health. It increases the blood supply to the brain, and can reduce depression, anxiety and stress. It also improves sleep.

I am a huge believer in its benefits. I used to exercise for the love of it — especially active sport (not least because it meant I could eat and drink without worrying about diet). Now I do it because I know I need to in order to stay healthy both physically and mentally.

The minimum prescribed by doctors seems to change as research moves the whole field of exercise on, but generally a 30-minute session, three times a week, seems to be the accepted minimum. The important thing is to make sure it is strenuous enough to get you out of breath, and make you sweat a bit. Find something you enjoy, so there is never a reason not to do something that enhances both your physical and mental wellbeing.

Diet

Diet again is very important, but is more personal to you than the other areas. The crucial thing is that it is well balanced and healthy (you know the drill, five portions of fruit and veg a day). If you are a vegetarian or vegan you will have your own requirements. Drinking plenty of water is important, especially if you are exercising regularly.

To attain — and retain — peak mental agility, focusing on foods that are best suited to brain performance obviously makes sense. Studies indicate that the five best categories of food for this are: leafy vegetables (kale, spinach); fatty fish (omega-3 fatty acids); berries; nuts; and finally, the good news — tea and coffee.

Light and nature

Plenty of daylight is now proven to be vital to health. Along with the Vitamin D boost of daylight, another outdoor benefit I have recently acquired is trees. Not going as far as hugging, but just standing among them. I am lucky enough to have a park opposite my office window, and if I need a break I find it very beneficial to walk over and look up into them. Some of them are very old, and very tall, and they bring a sense of timeless calm.

I have recently discovered people have been doing this for a long time in Japan, and around the world in recent years. Called Forest Bathing or *Shinrin-yoku*, it employs all the senses to achieve healing by enhancing wellbeing, reducing stress and restoring calm.

7. Affirmations

Affirmations are positive phrases or statements usually used to counterbalance the effects of self-sabotaging self-talk. All you need to do is pick a positive phrase and repeat it to yourself — either quietly or out loud.

There has been a move recently for some psychologists to doubt the effectiveness of affirmations. However, support in the neuroscientific research community is still strong. There is MRI evidence suggesting that certain neural pathways are increased when people practise self-affirmation tasks, and recent studies have shown they can increase physical performance and reduce stress.

The strong arm proof

Here is an exercise that will prove to you that positive thinking and affirmations work. It is what I call the Strong Arm Proof.

I've done this in front of audiences in conference halls, and with my own kids. It works anywhere. I ask a helpful volunteer to face the audience and hold one arm at right angles to the body, parallel to their shoulder.

I ask them to hold their arm out and to say loudly (and mean it), 'I am weak and I am unworthy.' I then tell them I am about to push their arm down, and they should resist with all their strength. When I try to push their arm down, *I can do it almost without effort.*

I then ask them to repeat ten times, loudly (and mean it), 'I am strong and I am worthy.' When I try to push their arm down, however hard I try, invariably I fail to do so.

You can do this in either order, and it always works. It might seem a bit frivolous, but it is a simple example of the science behind it: **that your body listens to what your brain is telling it.** I then suggest they do it at home, or among friends, to demonstrate the almost unbelievable effect of positive — or negative — affirmations.

I've seen this done in extreme sports too. One game involves a bunch of elite climbers to see who can hold on to a narrow ledge by only one finger for the longest time. When hearing their companions shouting 'You're falling off, you're falling off,' they tend to release their hold 10 to 20 seconds earlier than if they shout, 'You're holding on, you're holding on!' This is impressive in itself, but what makes it more impressive is the fact that rock climbers and mountaineers tend to be unusually strong mentally. If they weren't, they would surrender to the voice telling them to let go, and fall with alarming frequency.

Whether you think you can, or whether you think you can't, you're right.

Henry Ford

Henry Ford is the man credited with these wise words. He was a man who lived at a time when work and life had recognisable patterns. Patterns that repeated. His innovation that created a highly effective pattern was the continuous production line for manufacturing cars. It was creative, but it was linear.

Now things develop in a more complex, less linear, way. But they are a whole lot more interesting. We are indeed privileged to live in a time of rich potential for developing new ways of working, of learning, of contributing, and of being creative in the widest sense.

As the pace of change accelerates, it produces more challenges and more opportunities. To both, the most effective way to respond is with agility, flexibility and enthusiasm.

This is why attitude is so crucial. As Ford suggests, thinking that you can succeed in doing or achieving something, or thinking you will not succeed, is simply down to how you approach it.

A positive attitude says you can and will deliver the possibilities you can envisage, even if success may not be easy. It is the result of a growth mindset that is open to engaging positively with the world.

A negative attitude is part of having a fixed mindset. This is just how things are. Don't rock the boat. You can't change them. You are right not to even try.

A negative attitude is confirmation that you are stuck. You are immobile because you accept — probably wrongly — that is how things are, and they can't be changed. A positive attitude makes you mobile. You are agile: you believe — probably rightly — that you can change things.

And because you are enthusiastic and open to events and trends, you are, to an important extent, futureproofed. You can anticipate and respond appropriately.

So, believe you can. Because it's true: you can.

Learning points and To Do list

1. Take the 24-Hour Challenge. And stick with it, till you can stay consistently positive.

2. Try the Strong Arm Proof on a couple of people. Confirm the effectiveness of positive affirmations to empower yourself. And others.

3. Be a radiator, not a drain.

4. Take your sleep and health seriously.

5. Think you can, and you will.

**You don't have to see the whole staircase.
Just take the first step.**

Martin Luther King

Conclusion

Our daughter was standing in the hallway of our house, steadying a massive cake.

She had designed the metre-wide treat in the shape of the Innocent Smoothies logo, for impact, and to feed all 70 employees working there. This was part of her imaginative job application (coinciding with their sixth birthday).

Tansy had found the company at their festival and been overwhelmed by the big banner above the main stage that simply said, 'hello everyone'. It was so open, inclusive and generous that she decided there and then it was the company for her. Luckily, the cake was rapturously received and she got a foot in the door, answering the Banana Phone. By the time she left nine years later, the staff had grown to nearly four hundred, and she had progressed through various roles in the creative team to eventually become their Brand Guardian.

What immediately made her love her work was the sense of creativity, openness and fun. Importantly, the fun was coupled with a sense of worthwhile values that were intensely lived throughout the company. Those were (and are): Natural — their fruit drinks contained nothing but fruit, and their people were always open and very much themselves; Entrepreneurial (with a saying that 'if it's 80 per cent right, go for it'); Responsible (of course); Commercial (it's a business, despite their reputation for having fun); and Generous (with their time-share scheme and the 10 per cent of profits set aside for their Foundation to eliminate world hunger). Employees' annual assessments were based on how well they lived the values. In Tansy's words, 'They were in our bones, day in, day out. They were in the air.'

In 2008 there came a severe test of those values.

All companies have growing pains — challenges that test the mettle of its leaders. You just have to believe what you are doing is right, and carry on. Innocent, like Cobra Sports, was under-capitalised for the huge growth it was undergoing. It therefore went out to funders to both keep itself afloat, and to finance the next steps in its development. The adventure then became real.

Lehman Brothers went bust the day they went looking, and all chance of refinancing went out the window. Many people had to be made redundant. The founders rose to the occasion, and came through with flying colours. Everyone was kept in the loop. There was openness and humanity.

Tansy survived the cull, but those who had to leave spoke highly of their treatment, and continued to be ambassadors for Innocent. The culture meant they had strengthened growth mindsets, and could react with agility to change. Several went on to set up their own businesses then, and many have started businesses since.

I share the Innocent story as it shows that when you find work (or alternative income streams) that chimes with your values, that has a clear purpose — it can be both fulfilling and fun.

It also demonstrates that in the current environment — as then — agility is a very effective and necessary way to operate in any organisation. Being agile involves being open-minded, enthusiastic and resilient in the face of setbacks. It also involves being well-informed and interested so you can futureproof yourself. The fact that the Innocent founders are among the backers of the London Interdisciplinary School demonstrates they are now actively involved in ways to futureproof the next generation of workers.

Attitudinal groundwork

Gandhi demonstrated that changing a mindset can transform the life chances of millions. On a more humble scale, the Innocent story brings to life the benefits of resisting conventional and accepted thinking. It encapsulates many of the core lessons of the book: a growth mindset, creativity, futureproofing, sound principles and resilience that enables mental agility to continue under pressure.

Developing agility is crucial to operating effectively in any organisation, and in life in general. But it's an ongoing process. Over time, it does become easier — but only with effort. Remember the law of entropy? Without effort, life tends to lose order. The good news is that effort, in this case, is richly rewarded. Mental agility is satisfying because you feel on top of things. You feel more in control. This in itself reduces stress and creates more positive energy. It's a virtuous circle.

I'll leave you with a recap of some of the important points we've covered in the book. Please do revisit them whenever you need to ground yourself and reset your mind:

- **exercise self-compassion** — turn the inner voice from negative to positive
- **enhance your growth mindset** — work on flexibility, responding positively to change, and relishing new ideas
- **neoteny: think young** — unencumbered by accepted ideas and ways of operating
- **listen to your conscience**, which tells you what is right and what is wrong
- **keep updating your values** to plug into a relevant and motivating purpose
- **develop and retain enthusiasm**, whatever the setbacks
- **apply rigour and energy** to being well-informed, interested and interesting
- **think insight**, not just knowledge
- **create alternative income streams** to give yourself agency and choice
- **find or create work** that is fulfilling and worthwhile
- **dare to dream**
- **try living on less**
- **experience a Helper's High regularly**
- **develop a giving mindset**
- **be a radiator**
- **think you can, and you will**

Resources

Books

Mindset: Changing the way you think to fulfil your potential
by Carol Dweck (Robinson)

Mindgym: Achieve more by thinking differently
by Sebastian Bailey & Octavius Black (HarperOne)

The Hungry Spirit by Charles Handy (Arrow)

Do Breathe: Calm your mind. Find focus. Get stuff done
by Michael Townsend Williams (Do Books)

*The Life-Changing Magic of Tidying: A simple, effective way
to banish clutter forever* by Marie Kondo (Vermilion)

*The Gig Economy: The complete guide to getting better
work, taking more time off, and financing the life you want*
by Diane Mulcahy (Amacom)

The 100-Year Life: Living and working in an age of longevity
by Lynda Gratton and Andrew Scott (Bloomsbury)

The Gift: How the creative spirit transforms the world
by Lewis Hyde (Canongate)

Try Giving Yourself Away by David Dunn (Prentice Hall)

The Theory of Moral Sentiments by Adam Smith (Penguin Classics)

The Five Side Effects of Kindness: This book will make you feel better, be happier and live longer by David Hamilton (Hay House)

Man's Search for Meaning: The classic tribute to hope from the Holocaust by Viktor E. Frankl (Rider)

The Happy Manifesto: Make your organization a great workplace by Henry Stewart (Kogan Page)

The Anxiety Epidemic: The causes of our modern-day anxieties by Graham Davey (Robinson)

Hardwiring Happiness: How to reshape your brain and your life by Rick Hanson (Rider) and TEDx Talk

Online reading

The Four Future of Work Scenarios
thersa.org/discover/publications-and-articles/reports/the-four-futures-of-work-coping-with-uncertainty-in-an-age-of-radical-technologies

McKinsey Future of Work Studies
mckinsey.com/featured-insights/future-of-work/jobs-lost-jobs-gained-what-the-future-of-work-will-mean-for-jobs-skills-and-wages

Future of Work in America
mckinsey.org

Deloitte Global Millennial Survey 2021
deloitte.com/content/dam/Deloitte/global/Documents/2021-deloitte-global-millennial-survey-report.pdf

Online videos

Work/Life Balance, Marcus Child
  via YouTube.com

Guided Sleep Meditation, Deepak Chopra
  via YouTube.com

Perils of Perception, Ipsos
  ipsos.com/ipsos-mori/en-uk/perils-perception-2018

Hardwiring Happiness, Rick Hanson
  TedxMarin.org

The Tyranny of Merit, Michael Sandel
  thersa.org

Websites

The Centre for Compassion and Altruism Research
  and Education
  ccare.stanford.edu

The Centre for Mental Health
  www.centreformentalhealth.org.uk

About the Author

Tim Drake is a keynote speaker to business audiences around Europe on motivation and unlocking potential. He has co-founded and run businesses, think tanks and charities.

Now in his seventies, he believes that he, like most people, has more to give and more to learn. After 25 years, he still thrives in the shared learning his CEO Think Tanks provoke. Within each industry they are made up of members from all parts of the supply chain with the aim of rattling cages and keeping thinking open and agile.

He also recognises that challenges and setbacks are part of life and need to be addressed with courage, humour and a mindset based on resilience, gratitude, fairness and a desire to give back.

His previous publications include *Wearing the Coat of Change* (Orion, 1998), *How to Make a Difference* (Marshall Cavendish Business, 2012), *You Can Be as Young as You Think* (Pearson Prentice Hall Life, 2009) and *Generation Cherry* (Red Door, 2017). He gave a Do Lecture in 2012.

He is married with two grown up daughters, and lives in London.

Thanks

I would like to give profound thanks to my wife, Lizzie, for her consistent support and suggestions, aided by our daughter Lettice; to my daughter Tansy, for her inspired editing; and to Miranda, the guiding light of Do Books, for her wise, focused and enlightened overall editing of the book.

Index

Books in the series

Do Agile Tim Drake

Do Beekeeping Orren Fox

Do Birth Caroline Flint

Do Breathe
Michael Townsend Williams

Do Build Alan Moore

Do Deal
Richard Hoare & Andrew Gummer

Do Death Amanda Blainey

Do Design Alan Moore

Do Disrupt Mark Shayler

Do Drama Lucy Gannon

Do Earth Tamsin Omond

Do Fly Gavin Strange

Do Grow Alice Holden

Do Improvise Robert Poynton

Do Inhabit Sue Fan, Danielle Quigley

Do Lead Les McKeown

Do Listen Bobette Buster

Do Make James Otter

Do Open David Hieatt

Do Pause Robert Poynton

Do Photo Andrew Paynter

Do Present Mark Shayler

Do Preserve
Anja Dunk, Jen Goss, Mimi Beaven

Do Protect Johnathan Rees

Do Purpose David Hieatt

Do Scale Les McKeown

Do Sea Salt
Alison, David & Jess Lea-Wilson

Do Sing James Sills

Do Sourdough Andrew Whitley

Do Story Bobette Buster

Do Team Charlie Gladstone

Do Walk Libby DeLana

Do Wild Baking Tom Herbert

Also available

Path A short story about reciprocity Louisa Thomsen Brits

The Skimming Stone A short story about courage Dominic Wilcox

Stay Curious How we created a world class event in a cowshed Clare Hieatt

The Path of a Doer A simple tale of how to get things done David Hieatt

Available in print, digital and audio formats from booksellers or via our website: **thedobook.co**

To hear about events and forthcoming titles, you can find us on social media **@dobookco**, or subscribe to our newsletter